T0396063

Marie Curie
for Kids

Her Life and Scientific Discoveries

with 21 Activities and Experiments

Amy M. O'Quinn

CHICAGO REVIEW PRESS

Published by Chicago Review Press Incorporated
814 North Franklin Street
Chicago, Illinois 60610
ISBN 978-1-61373-320-2

Library of Congress Cataloging-in-Publication Data
Names: O'Quinn, Amy M.
Title: Marie Curie for kids : her life and scientific discoveries, with 21 activities and experiments / Amy M. O'Quinn.
Description: Chicago, Illinois : Chicago Review Press, Incorporated, [2017] | Includes bibliographical references
    and index.
Identifiers: LCCN 2016009405 (print) | LCCN 2016010172 (ebook) | ISBN 9781613733202 (pbk. : alk. paper)
    | ISBN 9781613733219 (pdf) | ISBN 9781613733233 (epub) | ISBN 9781613733226 (Kindle)
Subjects: LCSH: Curie, Marie, 1867-1934—Juvenile literature. | Women chemists—Poland—Biography—Juvenile literature.
    | Women chemists—France—Biography—Juvenile literature. | Nobel Prize winners—Biography—Juvenile literature.
    | Radioactivity—History—Juvenile literature.
Classification: LCC QD22.C8 O68 2017 (print) | LCC QD22.C8 (ebook) | DDC 540.92—dc23
LC record available at http://lccn.loc.gov/2016009405

Cover and interior design: Monica Baziuk
Interior illustrations/maps: Lindsey Cleworth Schauer
Cover images: Front cover (clockwise from left): Marie in her lab, Musée Curie (coll. ACJC); technician
X-raying wounded soldier, National World War I Museum and Memorial, Kansas City, Missouri, USA; Pierre Curie,
source unknown; hand X-ray, Jayakumar, Shutterstock; Marie and Irène Curie, Musée Curie (coll. ACJC); Pierre Curie's
radioactivity measuring device, photo Cecile Charré/Institut Curie. Back cover (clockwise from top): Marie Curie, 1888,
Musée Curie (coll. ACJC); the Sorbonne, author's collection; glowing radium, Musée Curie (coll. ACJC).

Printed in the United States of America
5 4 3

For my family

CONTENTS

TIME LINE

1859 ❋ Pierre Curie is born on May 15

1867 ❋ Marie Curie is born on November 7

1876 ❋ Marie's oldest sister, Zosia, dies from typhus

1878 ❋ Marie's mother, Bronisława, dies from tuberculosis

1884–90 ❋ Marie works as a governess

1891 ❋ Marie moves to Paris to attend the Sorbonne

1894 ❋ Marie meets Pierre

1895 ❋ Pierre and Marie get married

1897 ❋ Irène Curie is born

1898 ❋ Marie discovers polonium and, later, radium

❋ Marie and Pierre begin working to isolate uranium salts

1903 ❋ Marie earns her doctorate

❋ Marie and Pierre share the Nobel Prize in Physics with Henri Becquerel

1904 ❋ Ève Curie is born

1906 ❋ Pierre Curie is killed in a street accident

❋ Marie becomes the first female professor with a chair position at the Sorbonne

1911 ❋ Marie wins her second Nobel Prize, this time in Chemistry

1912 ❋ Construction on the Radium Institute begins

1914 ❋ The Radium Institute is completed, and World War I begins

1915–18 ❋ Marie organizes and operates mobile
radiology units during World War I

1921 ❋ Marie and her daughters visit the United
States to receive a gift of radium

1926 ❋ Irène marries Frédéric Joliot

1929 ❋ Marie visits the United States to receive a monetary gift to buy
radium for a Polish radium treatment and research facility

1932 ❋ The Maria Skłodowska-Curie Institute
officially opens in Warsaw, Poland

1934 ❋ Irène and Frédéric discover artificial radioactivity
❋ Marie dies of pernicious anemia in the French Alps on July 4

1935 ❋ Irène and Frédéric win a Nobel Prize in Chemistry
for their discovery of artificial radioactivity

1995 ❋ Marie and Pierre are reburied at the Panthéon in Paris

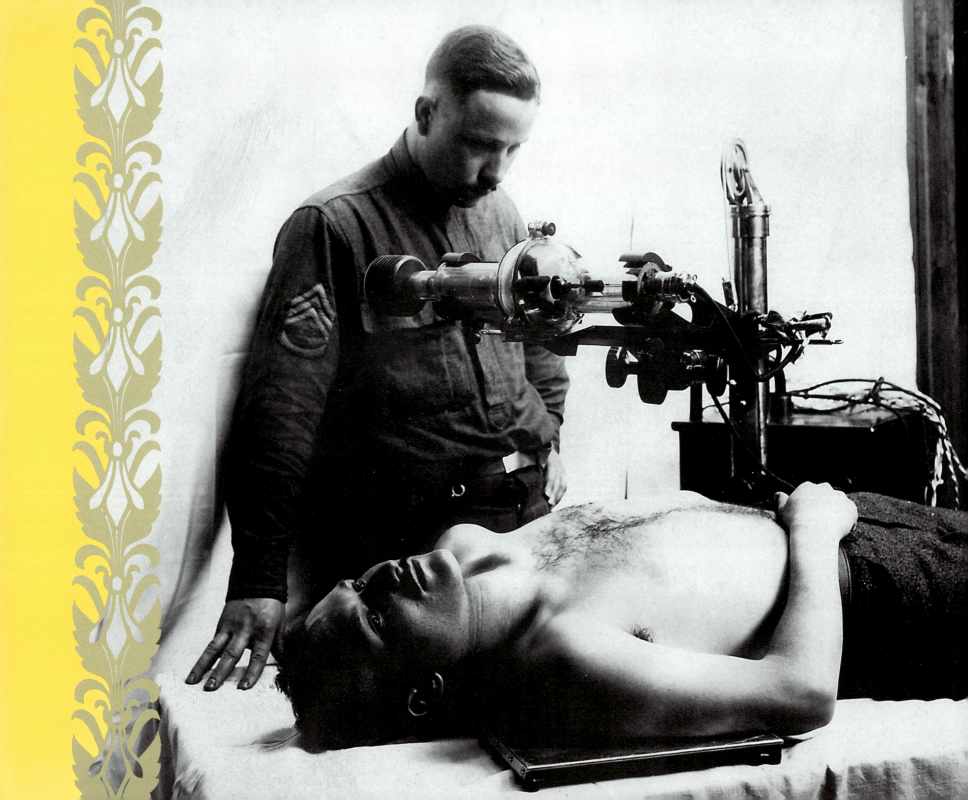

INTRODUCTION

The fourth-class railway carriage clacked down the track as a young Polish woman in a threadbare coat crouched down on a folding chair in the middle of the train car, her luggage gathered closely around her. Though the landscape and car were dark in the night, her soul was illuminated with excitement and anticipation as the carriage made its way toward France. She'd waited so long for this! What would Paris be like? Could she make it at the Sorbonne? What would her future hold?

Her plan was to return home to Poland after graduation, find a teaching position in her field, spread ideas of liberation to her fellow Poles, and hopefully see her beloved country become free once again. So how could she have ever imagined the very different path her life would take and the dramatic events that would unfold? How could she have foreseen the trials, setbacks, love, heartaches, and successes that awaited her at the other end of the track? She didn't realize that the journey she was beginning would lead her to becoming one of the world's most important scientists.

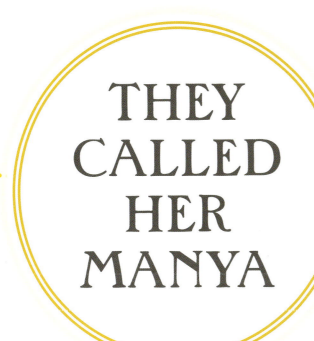

THEY CALLED HER MANYA

1

"Beg—pardon! Pardon! I didn't do it on purpose. It's not my fault—it's not Bronya's fault! It's only because it was so easy!" the four-year-old cried.

The little girl had jumped up to read aloud from a schoolbook only when her older sister Bronya faltered while doing a simple reading lesson. Yet the silence, then the shocked expressions on her parents' faces and the sulky glance from Bronya, caused her to panic. What had she done? Were they displeased with her even though she found reading, and all learning, to be almost effortless? And why was her sister upset, when Bronya was the one who had wanted to play teacher with her in the first place?

> All my life through,
> the new sights
> of Nature made me
> rejoice like a child.
>
> —MARIE CURIE

The year was 1871. The little girl didn't understand that her parents, both experienced teachers, followed the mindset of the times. Although they valued education, they believed that encouraging learning and mental development in very young children was not wise. While they were proud of their daughter's abilities, they didn't want her acting older than her age. When she yearned to play with her father's scientific instruments, kept in a glass case, they told her to play with her blocks or her doll. When she reached for one of the many books in the house, they instructed her to sing a song or go into the garden.

However, the child was curious and interested in everything around her. She was like a sponge, constantly soaking up knowledge and new ideas. She simply could not stop learning. In fact, she would grow up to be recognized as one of the most brilliant and famous women of all time—Marie Curie.

Manya and Her Family

MARIA SALOMEA Skłodowska was born on November 7, 1867, on Freta Street in Warsaw, Poland. Nicknamed Manya by her family, she was the youngest of five children born to

Marie Curie's birthplace in Warsaw, Poland, now the Maria Skłodowska-Curie Museum.

Bronisława and Vladisłav Skłodowski.[*] She had three sisters and a brother, and they too had affectionate pet names or "diminutives" commonly used in Poland by family members and close friends. The oldest child, Sophia, was known as Zosia. Bronisława, named for her mother, was nicknamed Bronya, and Helena was referred to as Hela. Manya's only brother, Joseph, was called Jozio. All the Skłodowski children were quite intelligent. Their home was full of laughter, good books, and poetry. Yet of all her siblings, Manya seemed to possess the most remarkable and unusual attention span and concentration skills.

Manya's mother, Bronisława, had been born into a family of former minor-nobility land owners. Although Bronisława's parents, Felix and Maria Boguski, were once considered to be upper class, they had lost most of their land over the years due to invasions by other countries. Left without land or wealth, they managed the properties of others.

Despite having little money, the Boguskis still found a way to send Bronisława and her sisters to a private girls' school in Warsaw called the Freta Street School, where she received a very good education. In time Bronisława would become a teacher there and eventually the headmistress. The position provided a home for her family to live in, and she

kept the job for several years, even after she was married and had children.

Bronisława was a skilled pianist with a lovely singing voice. Indeed, she was a very beautiful, accomplished, and graceful woman. She was also a pious and devout Catholic and an attentive mother, and Manya loved her dearly.

[*] In Slavic languages, such as Polish, -ski is the masculine suffix and -ska is the feminine suffix.

Manya's father, Vładisław, was also from a family of Polish minor nobility. One of his ancestors had owned several hundred acres of land and lived a very comfortable life as a well-to-do farmer, as did many of his descendants. Unfortunately, this was not the case for Vładisław's father, Joseph. So, with a desire to improve his circumstances and honor the family name, Vładisław chose to focus on study and academics. He became the director of a boys' school in Lublin and is credited as being the first intellectual in the Skłodowski family.

Like his father, Vładisław attended the University of Petersburg in Russia and excelled in scientific studies. He returned to Warsaw, where he became a professor of mathematics and **physics**, and married Bronisława in 1860. Everyone agreed that it was a "very suitable" marriage. And given their intelligence and fierce loyalty to their Polish roots, their children would be not only well educated but also taught to honor their heritage.

▲ **ABOVE:** The Skłodowski siblings. Left to right, Sophia (Zosia), Helena (Hela), Maria (Manya), Joseph (Jozio), and Bronisława (Bronya). Musée Curie (coll. ACJC))

◄ **LEFT:** Bronisława Skłodowska, Marie Curie's mother. **RIGHT:** Vładisław Skłodowski, Marie Curie's father. Musée Curie (coll. ACJC)

Russia-Controlled Poland

WHY WAS it so important to Manya's parents to teach their children the history and culture of their own country? Surely they would be taught these things in school, right?

Actually, Poland had once been one of the most powerful countries in Europe, but in 1772, Russia, Prussia (now Germany), and Austria had seized control of most of the land and divided it among themselves. The name *Poland* was completely removed from the map.

The French military leader Napoleon Bonaparte tried to help the Poles form a small Polish state in the early 1800s, but he was defeated by the Russians, and the land reverted right back to Russian czar Alexander I, whose troops now occupied the country. The czar decided the time had come to crack down even harder on the Poles, and the "Russification" of Poland began.

New laws required that Poles learn the Russian language and customs. Poles were no longer allowed to celebrate their own religions, culture, and history or teach these to their children. The Russians wanted to completely strip them of their Polish identities and erase any traces of their former lives. Anyone who dared to do things the "old" way or was caught speaking Polish was punished severely. The Poles were also the targets of discrimination, and all the best jobs went to Russians and those who supported the czar.

The loyal Polish people were furious! Two times they rebelled and tried to overthrow their oppressors—in 1830 and again in 1863. But their efforts failed, and anyone who took part in the rebellions suffered the consequences. Families lost land, and some Poles were sent away, put in prison, or worse. Manya's paternal grandfather, Joseph Skłodowski, had taken part in the 1830 uprising and was captured. Although he was finally released, he never got his land back, and a hatred for the Russians was passed down in his family through the generations.

Life Changes

MANYA'S FATHER, Vladislav, had had his own problems with the Russians. In 1868, he made some school officials where he worked very angry—probably because of his Polish loyalty and the regular discrimination against the Poles—and was fired from his job. He was soon able to find another teaching position in a Warsaw boys' school, which provided an apartment for the family. Bronisława resigned from her job as headmistress of the Freta Street School, and the Skłodowskis moved into their new quarters not long after Manya was born.

Bronisława was talented and hardworking, and, now as a full-time homemaker, she put

Learn About Poland's Geography

WHEN MANYA WAS BORN in 1867, Poland did not exist on the map. It had been conquered and divided up between Russia, Germany, and Austria years earlier. Look at the map below to see the boundary lines of the three empires that controlled Polish land in the late 1800s. The Poland of today is outlined between the three other countries. Notice that Manya's home city of Warsaw was in the area ruled by Russia.

Poland is much different than it was in 1867, and even the countries surrounding it have changed somewhat. Map Manya's beloved native country as it today.

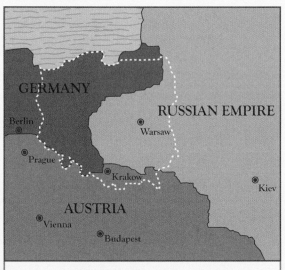

Poland was divided between Russia, Austria, and Germany when Marie Curie was born in 1867.

You'll Need

※ Current map of Poland
※ Paper
※ Pen or marker

Photocopy or trace the map of Poland below or download and print a PDF at https://commons .wikimedia.org/wiki/File%3APoland_map_blank .png.

Use an atlas to identify the location of the bordering countries and the Baltic Sea and label these. Mark and label the following cities: Gdansk, Krakow, Lodz, Poznan, Szczuki, Warsaw, and Wroclaw. Draw and label the Oder and Vistula Rivers. Mark and label the Carpathian Mountains.

all her energy into caring for her family and home. She even learned to make their shoes herself in order to save money! Because of her mother's example, Manya never hesitated to do manual labor or dirty work as she grew up.

On the other hand, Manya did not remember ever being hugged or kissed by her mother, but it was less common at the time for parents to openly display affection. Manya was content to cling to her mother's skirt or feel Bronisława's gentle caress on her hair or face. However, when Manya was about five years old, Bronisława became careful about touching her husband and children and started keeping her eating utensils and plates separate from the rest of the family's. Manya was confused; she didn't know that her mother had contracted a deadly and highly contagious disease called **tuberculosis**. The children remembered their mother's attacks of dry coughing, as well as their daily prayers to "restore our mother's health."

Not wanting to upset her family, Bronisława carried on with her duties without complaining or calling attention to her sickness. She did, however, make a yearlong trip to a clinic in the South of France for a rest cure, in hopes of getting better. Zosia went with her. Unfortunately, the rest did not help. About the time they returned back home, Vladislav lost his job and they had to move again.

Infectious Diseases 𝕯

Both Marie Curie's mother and sister died from infectious diseases—Bronisława from tuberculosis and Zosia from typhus.

Tuberculosis (also called consumption many years ago) is caused by the bacteria *Mycobacterium tuberculosis,* which primarily attacks the lungs. People with weakened immune systems have a higher risk of contracting the disease, which can be spread when an infected person coughs or sneezes and the bacteria becomes airborne. If another person breathes in that bacteria, they too can become infected, as was the case for Marie's mother. Symptoms may include a bad cough that lasts several weeks, chest pain, coughing up blood, fatigue, weight loss, fever, chills, and night sweats. The first tuberculosis vaccine was developed in 1921 by two French microbiologists, Albert Calmette and Camille Guérin.

Typhus is caused by a bacteria called *Rickettsia prowazekii,* which can be carried by contaminated lice, ticks, or fleas. This epidemic form of the disease is spread by bites from these parasitic insects. Symptoms may include high fever, chills, rash, joint and muscle pain, sensitivity to light, delirium, or confusion. Typhus is not to be confused with typhoid fever, a bacterial disease contracted by consuming contaminated food or water. Typhus can also occur in places where sanitary conditions are bad, and cases are rare in the United States. The first effective typhus vaccine was developed by Rudolf Weigl, a Polish research biologist, in the late 1930s and early 1940s.

The family tried to make ends meet by taking in boarders. This seemed a good solution until one of them introduced another dreaded disease into the household—**typhus**. Both Zosia and Bronya became sick, and Zosia never recovered. Her death was a blow to the whole family. And when Bronisława, who had never fully recovered from tuberculosis, passed away two years later, 10-year-old Manya was devastated. The heartbreak of losing both her sister and her mother in such a short time affected her deeply.

School Days

DESPITE THE sad events at home, Manya excelled at school. Alexander II was now the czar, and the Russian government controlled the schools. Teachers were supposed to give lessons on the Russian language, religion, culture, and history, and any teacher who dared to speak Polish, give instruction in Polish history or literature, or encourage any type of patriotism would be fired and punished. In order to make sure these orders were carried out, inspectors made school visits frequently.

Many Poles pretended allegiance to the foreign government and guarded their words and actions in public while still speaking, honoring, and teaching Polish ways in their own homes. Like Manya's family, they dreamed of a day when they would all be free again. But, for now, they had to be careful, because there were spies everywhere just waiting for the chance to turn someone in.

But there were also some brave teachers who dared to quietly rebel and teach Polish history and literature in their classrooms. They had a warning system in place to alert them if a Russian inspector made a surprise visit. Manya remembered one terrifying inspection in particular.

When she was about 10 years old, she attended a private Polish school. Because she was bright and had advanced so quickly, she was almost two years younger than the other girls in her class. One of Manya's favorite teachers was Miss Tupalska, who was nicknamed "Tupsia." Tupsia looked stern and maintained a strict and orderly classroom, but she was also a quiet Polish rebel who secretly instructed her young students in Polish history, along with their regular Russian-approved lessons in math and history.

One day during a Polish history lesson, the special warning bell alerted them that a Russian inspector was coming. Quickly, some of the girls grabbed the forbidden books and rushed them into another building before hurrying back to the classroom, where the others now sat quietly sewing. Tupsia was reading aloud in Russian from a book of Russian fairy tales.

The inspector, Mr. Hornberg, entered the room and looked around suspiciously. He lifted the top of a nearby desk to peer inside. Nothing. Then he commanded the teacher to ask one of the students to recite for him. Manya knew she would be chosen, because her Russian was flawless and she always knew the drills. Yet how she hated it, even as she stood ready to play her part and protect her teacher and her classmates.

Make Pierogies: A Polish Treat

THERE ARE ALL KINDS of delicious traditional Polish foods, and one of the most famous is the pierogi. This is a large dumpling that can be filled with different ingredients such as cheese, meat, potatoes, or fruit. The traditional pierogi dough is made from flour, water, salt, oil, and sometimes eggs. But you can take a shortcut and make pierogies from wonton wrappers. Fill with blueberries, powdered sugar, and cream cheese for a quick, delicious treat.

Adult supervision required

You'll Need

※ 2 cups (300 g) blueberries (sweetened with extra sugar if necessary)
※ 6 ounces (170 g) cream cheese, softened
※ Pinch of salt
※ 1 cup (100 g) powdered sugar, plus more for sprinkling
※ 1 teaspoon (3 g) cinnamon (optional)
※ 12 wonton wrappers
※ 1 egg white, lightly beaten
※ 1–2 tablespoons (15–30 g) butter
※ Whipped cream (optional)
※ Large pot
※ Colander
※ Mixing bowl
※ Hand mixer
※ Rubber spatula or wooden spoon

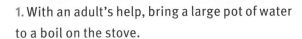

※ Cutting board
※ 3-inch (8-cm) metal biscuit cutter
※ Pastry brush
※ Large nonstick skillet
※ Slotted spoon
※ Paper towels

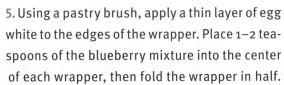

1. With an adult's help, bring a large pot of water to a boil on the stove.

2. Using clean hands, crush the blueberries in a bowl and then *drain extremely well* in a colander (this step is crucial, or the filling will be too runny). Sweeten with a bit of sugar if needed. Set aside.

3. With a hand mixer, blend room-temperature cream cheese, salt, powdered sugar, and cinnamon (if desired) together until smooth. Gently fold in crushed blueberries with a spatula or spoon. (Be careful not to overmix.) Add a bit more powdered sugar if the mixture is too soupy. Set mixture aside.

4. Lay a wonton wrapper on a cutting board and, using the biscuit cutter, cut a circle from it. Do this for all 12 wrappers.

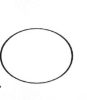

5. Using a pastry brush, apply a thin layer of egg white to the edges of the wrapper. Place 1–2 teaspoons of the blueberry mixture into the center of each wrapper, then fold the wrapper in half. Press the edges to seal the dumpling. (You can crimp the edges with a fork as well.)

6. With an adult's help and supervision, carefully place the pierogies into the pot of boiling water and let them cook for 2–3 minutes, or until they float. Using a slotted spoon, remove the pierogies from the pot and rinse them with cool water in a colander. Drain the pierogies well.

7. Again with an adult's help, melt the butter in a nonstick skillet over medium heat. Carefully place the pierogies in the hot butter and brown for 2–3 minutes on each side or until golden. Remove each dumpling with a slotted spoon and drain on paper towels. Let them cool completely before serving.

Optional
Sprinkle more powdered sugar on top of the pierogies and/or serve them with whipped cream.

When Mr. Hornberg asked her to recite her prayer, she did so in perfect Russian, even though it was humiliating. When he drilled her on the long list of former Russian rulers, their titles, and the names of the current imperial family, she knew them all.

However, when he asked, "Who rules over us?" Manya did not answer immediately. The inspector grew irritated and loudly asked the question again. He obviously did not care that the little girl before him was suffering.

Finally, she answered painfully, "His Majesty Alexander II, Tsar of all the Russias."

The inspection was over, and Mr. Hornberg left. Tupsia kissed Manya's forehead, and the little girl burst into tears. The stress of leading a double life was terrible for adults, but it was almost unbearable for children. They detested the Russians and their traitorous Polish supporters. Manya and her friends actually made a habit of spitting at the monument dedicated "To the Poles faithful to their Sovereign" in Saxony Square every time they passed by.

Despite the strain of inspections, Manya excelled in her studies, as did her siblings. Jozio and Bronya graduated first in their high school classes and each received the gold medal, a prize awarded to the top student. They both wanted to become doctors, and Jozio was able to attend the University of Warsaw. But for Bronya and other women in Russia-controlled Poland in the late 1800s, there was no opportunity for higher education. In fact, there were very few schools in any countries that admitted females. The Sorbonne in France was one that did, but first Bronya would have to work and save money.

As for Manya, she was a brilliant student who showed particular strengths in math and science. It was no surprise when she too graduated at the top of her class from the Russian

Alexander II, circa 1870.
The Di Rocco Wieler Private Collection, Toronto, Canada

high school on June 12, 1883. At the age of 15, she netted the third gold medal for the family. Now she had to decide what to do next.

Yet, soon after graduation, Manya became ill. A smart but very sensitive girl, she was prone to depression and suffered from a nervous condition that seemed to affect her most when she was overly tired or stressed. Her father decided she needed a change of scenery and made plans for her and her sister Hela to take a year off to visit with relatives in the Polish countryside. It was time for Manya to rest and relax.

Vladislav with his daughters (left to right) Manya, Bronya, and Hela in 1890. Musée Curie (coll. ACJC)

YEARNING FOR MORE

2

It seems that life is not easy for any of us. But what of that? We must have perseverance and above all confidence in ourselves. We must believe that we are gifted for something and that this thing must be attained.

—MARIE CURIE, IN A LETTER TO HER BROTHER, JOZIO, 1887

Weary in spirit and mentally exhausted, Manya looked forward to time off from academics and work at home. And since many of her aunts and uncles had homes in the Polish countryside, there were many places for her to visit. For the first time in her life, Manya was able to do just as she pleased with no thoughts of disease, tests, housework, or schedules. If she wanted to be lazy and sleep until ten o'clock in the morning, no one objected. If she wanted to play games, walk in the woods, swim, ride horses, or spend her day reading "harmless and absurd little novels," it was her choice. At long last, she simply enjoyed life.

Manya and Hela went from one set of relatives to another, often staying weeks at a time at one home before moving on to the next. At one point she wrote to her best friend Kazia Przyborovaska, "I can't believe geometry or algebra ever existed. I have completely forgotten them."

It was during this year of rest and pleasure that Manya discovered a passion that would last her whole life. She fell in love with nature and the countryside. She delighted in the changing of the seasons, the sight of the Carpathian Mountains in the distance, and her discovery of the beauty all around in her beloved Polish land.

Manya enjoyed other pastimes that year. In the winter, she and Hela stayed with their father's brother, Uncle Zdzislav, and his family at their home in the Carpathian Mountains. The cold evenings were spent merrymaking and dancing—with one **kulig** party after another.

A kulig was not just an ordinary party. It was an exciting, magical adventure! Manya and her companions, masked and dressed as peasant girls, hopped into sleighs pulled by magnificent horses and were escorted by young men in traditional Polish clothing wielding dazzling torches. Huddling under blankets to ward off the cold, Manya and the others enjoyed the late-night ride and lively tunes played by Jewish musicians who followed in another sleigh, fiddling all the while.

As they traveled along, more and more sleighs joined the party as others answered the call of the spirited music and joyful crowd. When the procession halted, the young people hopped from the sleighs and ran to pound on the door of a designated house. The owner, pretending to be surprised, opened the door, and the whole crowd noisily surged inside to dance and partake of delicious food that had been prepared far in advance.

Then at a given signal, everyone hastily exited the home, leaped back into the sleighs, and headed to the next house for more dancing, fun, and food. On and on, the *farandole*, or chain of sleighs, sped through the night, celebrating at additional houses, gaining more revelers at each stop. As dawn broke, Manya and her fellow merrymakers snatched a bit of sleep wherever they could find a place to lay their heads before heading off again.

On the second night, the procession finally stopped in front of the largest house in the neighborhood, where the "real" ball was to be held. Sixteen-year-old Manya, in her pretty costume and considered one of the best dancers present, didn't lack for partners. She had a grand time, and in an enthusiastic letter to Kazia, she shared, "I have been to a kulig. You can't imagine how delightful it is, especially when the clothes are beautiful and the boys are well dressed. My costume was very pretty."

Create a Nature Journal and Observation Kit

MANYA LOVED TO STUDY nature and make observations about the great outdoors. (These skills would serve her well as a scientist keeping lab notebooks one day.) She especially enjoyed the changing of the seasons and the area around the Carpathian Mountains where she spent a year after finishing high school.

By creating your own nature journal and kit for carrying your observation tools and supplies, you can be a student of nature too and keep a record of the things you observe.

You'll Need

* 5 brown paper lunch bags
* Scissors
* Stapler
* Washi tape
* Glue
* Markers or pens
* Magazine photos, scrapbook paper, and/or other printed designs (optional)
* 9 sheets of 8½-by-11-inch (A4) white paper
* Paper clips

1. Stack five brown paper lunch bags on top of each other, alternating open ends. Fold the stack in half and staple along the folded edge to create a booklet. Use colorful washi tape to cover up the stapled edge. Glue down any bag-bottom flaps on the inside pages so each page is flat.

2. Using markers or pens, decorate the front of your nature journal with your own choice of design and text.

3. Next, cut the sheets of white paper into halves, along the short edge, forming 18 rectangles. Glue one rectangle onto each page opening inside your journal. This will give you a clean, white space for drawing and writing.

4. The bag openings can be used as pockets for collecting specimens or samples. Use paper clips to keep the pockets closed when filled.

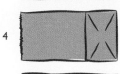
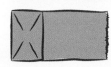

5. Now gather useful items for recording things you see, smell, hear, or touch in nature. These could include a magnifying glass, binoculars, a ruler, collection canisters, tweezers, colored pencils, pens, or markers. Store the items along with your journal in a carryall bag or backpack. This will be your nature observation kit.

Strap on your kit whenever you go on a hike, camping, on vacation, or even on a walk around your neighborhood, and you'll always be ready to write or sketch your thoughts and observations as well as collect samples of what you see, such as leaves, flowers, seeds, and so on.

With such freedom and carefree days to spend as she wished, Manya felt young and happy. All the sadness and dark days of her early childhood seemed far away. She loved being with her cousins and new friends, and life was a celebration. In fact, she would always remember these days as some of the happiest of her life. But it was time to go home.

Back to Work

AFTER MANYA'S year of travel and fun, she returned to Warsaw. Her oldest sister Bronya had been shouldering the responsibilities of home while she and Hela had been away. And although Manya had enjoyed her year of relaxation, she had missed her father and Bronya. The bond she shared with the two of them was strong, and they certainly influenced her values and early direction in life more than anyone else.

Vładisłav was not a wealthy man, yet he gave his children opportunities to learn within a rich intellectual environment. He kept up with the latest scientific discoveries in the areas of **chemistry** and physics. He expected his children to know Greek and Latin and to speak several foreign languages. He shared poetry and read aloud great literature—especially the finest writings of Polish authors, most of which were forbidden by Russian law.

Through his teachings and discussions, Manya's father was broadening the minds of his children, but he was also reinforcing their love and loyalty for Poland and a dream of nationhood. And like many other oppressed citizens, Manya and her siblings were willing to put aside personal ambitions to do whatever they could to help advance their fellow countrymen and free Poland from Russia's stranglehold.

Try Your Hand at Wycinanki: Polish Paper Cutting

POLAND HAS MANY FASCINATING cultural traditions, including the art of *wycinanki* (pronounced vee-chee-non-kee), which means "paper cut design" in Polish. Wycinanki dates back to the mid-1800s, and, as with dance costumes, designs vary depending on the region where the artist lives. The process usually involves complex paper folds and many tiny snips and cuts using special scissors to create designs that are often elaborate and intricate. Birds, flowers, and snowflakes are all popular designs for wycinanki artists. Try your hand (and skill) with this simplified snowflake paper cut design.

You'll Need
※ 1 sheet 8½-by-11-inch (A4) white paper
※ Pencil
※ Small, sharp scissors (manicure scissors will work)

1. Cut the paper into an 8½-by-8½-inch (210-by-210-mm for A4) square.

2. Fold the paper square in half diagonally three times, as shown in the diagram below:

> From corner A to corner B.
> From corner C to corner D.
> From corner E to corner F.

Make sure you keep track of the corner that's at the center of the square paper when unfolded. You can put a small pencil dot in that corner as a reminder not to cut there.

3. Draw shapes along the edges of the triangular folded paper and use scissors to cut along the lines of your design.

4. Unfold the paper carefully to reveal your finished wycinanki snowflake.

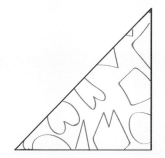

Optional
Once you've mastered the snowflake, why not try a more intricate design, such as a flower or bird? You can use colored construction paper instead of white paper or use markers and paint to decorate your final wycinanki creation.

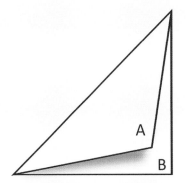

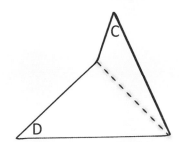

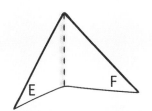

Manya became associated with a group called Positivists, who passionately believed that one way to do this was to build Polish intellect and educate the poor. This desire for intellectual advancement began to move away from the artistic and literary and toward the scientific. Chemistry, physics, hard sciences—the era of scientific advancement was quickly approaching.

During this time, Manya tried to help support her family financially by giving private lessons to schoolchildren. She quickly learned that this line of work could be tiring, thankless, and frustrating, especially when parents conveniently forgot to pay the few rubles she counted on receiving.

However, some Positivist associates introduced Manya to the Flying (or Floating) University, where she and Bronya began taking classes. This secret school provided classes for young people who wanted to further their education. In turn, the students were supposed to become educators. The Flying University classes were usually taught by Polish professors and teachers. Participation was dangerous, and, if discovered, students and teachers might face imprisonment.

Because they were women, Manya and Bronya were not allowed to attend college in Poland, as their brother Jozio did. They were just thankful for any opportunity for higher learning, even though the system had its problems and limitations. At this point in their lives, the Flying University classes were the best the sisters could hope for while still living in Poland.

The Governess

MORE THAN anything, Manya's sister Bronya wanted to be a doctor, but of course, this career path was closed to a Polish woman living in Russia-controlled Warsaw. However, it *was* possible for her to attend the Sorbonne in Paris, which had begun admitting women in 1860. The problem was that she only had

The Flying University 🎧

In 1882, the Flying (or Floating) University was started to provide secret classes for Polish women who wanted higher education but had no way to get it. They were taught in private homes around Warsaw by Polish professors and teachers who were part of the Positivist movement. Students could take classes in anatomy, natural history, or sociology. However, if any of the teachers or students had been caught, they would have been arrested.

Later, in 1885, the Flying University included both male and female students. The classes were taught at a building called the Museum of Industry and Agriculture, but this name was simply a cover to keep the Russians from finding out about the Polish-based education that was taking place inside. Manya's cousin Joseph Boguski was the museum's director, and some of the best Polish professors taught classes. There was even a small laboratory where Manya could do scientific research. The Flying University lasted until 1905, at which time the participants were finally allowed to start legal activities. The Flying University eventually transformed into the Society of Science Courses.

enough money saved to pay for one year of college. But 17-year-old Manya came up with a plan to help Bronya pursue her dream—an alliance of sorts.

Manya would become a governess and send most of her earnings to Bronya in Paris. With a bit of additional money that their father provided and her own savings, Bronya would have enough to attend the Sorbonne. Then after Bronya became a doctor, she would help put Manya through school.

It was a good plan, but at first Bronya would not hear of it. She felt guilty. She couldn't bear the thought of her younger sister working for what could end up being years as a governess while she lived and studied in Paris. She questioned the fairness of the plan. Finally, however, Manya talked her into it, saying, "Oh Bronya, don't be stupid! Because you are twenty and I'm seventeen. Because you've been waiting for hundreds of years and I've got lots of time."

Reluctantly, Bronya agreed and set off for Paris, while Manya left for a governess post in Szczuki, about 50 miles north of Warsaw. It was a big sacrifice for Manya to leave her family and head into the unknown. Yet the pay was good at 500 rubles a year, and she intended to keep her end of the alliance with her sister.

Manya, 1888. Musée Curie (coll. ACJC)

Manya's new employers, the Zorawski family, were well off, but not rich. Their home was an old-fashioned villa, but Manya's room faced a sugar beet factory in which Monsieur Zorawski, an "agriculturist of repute," held a great number of shares. Manya, who had imagined beautiful rural landscapes, saw nothing but sugar beets filling the great, monotonous plain in front of her.

However, she liked the family and the girls she cared for, Bronka (18 years old) and Andzia (10 years old), and thought she had done quite well financially in securing her position. The Zorawskis also had three sons in Warsaw

Life as a Governess ♪♪

Up until the outbreak of World War I, it was common for wealthy European families to employ a governess to teach their children in their homes, especially if they lived in the countryside or some distance from a suitable school. The role of governess required a young lady to be well educated, understand proper etiquette, come from a good middle-class family, and be of high moral character. Her behavior and reputation had to be absolutely flawless. The station of a governess was above the servant class, yet the governess was not considered the equal of the family she served. This often put the young lady in a difficult, and lonely, position. Although a governess poured time and effort into her pupils, she could be looked down upon or taken for granted.

A governess lived with the family and educated the children on all the subjects normally taught in schools. She was expected to be fluent in other languages in order to teach those as well. French was especially popular. For girl pupils, the program usually included art, music, and sewing. Boys were taught at home only until they were old enough to go away to a boarding school, or sometimes their education would be taken over by a male tutor. Some governesses stayed with their female pupils for years.

If a governess got married, she gave up her position. But it was difficult to meet suitable young men since she was neither a servant nor a socialite. Moreover, a governess's salary was not very high, and there was no retirement fund. Sadly, a former governess might find herself with no position or savings at middle age.

The Governess, an oil painting by British artist Emily Mary Osborn (1828–1925), depicts the attitude some employers showed toward their governesses in the late 1800s. Wikimedia Commons

whom Manya had not met (one at the university and two in boarding schools). And in addition to Bronka and Andzia, there were two more, younger children in the home who were still too young for school.

In April she wrote to her cousin Henrietta, "The Z. household is relatively cultivated. Mr. Z. is an old-fashioned man, but full of good sense, sympathetic and reasonable. His wife is rather difficult to live with, but when one knows how to take her she is quite nice. I think she likes me well enough."

Manya settled into a routine. In addition to working with Andzia, who could often be contrary and lazy, she decided to set up a secret school for the village children to teach them the Polish language and history. This allowed Manya to enact her Positivist view of "enlightening the people." Despite the danger, the older Zorawski daughter, Bronka, was also immediately taken with the idea and wanted to assist.

Manya used her own savings to purchase copybooks and pens for her new students. These sons and daughters of servants, farmers, and factory workers often were dirty, and some were sullen and inattentive. But in many, Manya could see a great desire in their eyes to learn to read and write. She was very moved by the children's pride in their accomplishments and by their mostly illiterate parents' admiration for them.

Despite her overall satisfaction with her situation, however, after two years of hard work, 19-year-old Manya started feeling despondent. Already prone to depression, she began to doubt that she would ever escape her fate as a governess buried in a remote part of Poland, and actually go to France to study. It was not that she believed Bronya would fail to keep her end of the bargain—rather, she felt discouraged at the realization that her father would soon need her care.

Yet, despite her claims to others that she had no future ambition, Manya sat at her desk each night reading borrowed volumes of sociology and physics or corresponding with her father about mathematics. It was a contradiction of words and actions, but with a stubborn will, she continued to learn and educate herself.

First Love— and Disappointment

NOT LONG after her latest bout with depression, Manya's life changed once again. The eldest Zorawski son, Casimir, came home from Warsaw for the holidays. Once there, he discovered that his siblings' governess was a "fresh, graceful girl, with lovely skin and hair, fine wrists and slender ankles," "ash-gray eyes," and an intense gaze. She was an intriguing, pretty young lady "who could dance

marvelously, row and skate; who was witty and had nice manners; who could make up verses as easily as she rode a horse or drove a carriage; who was different… totally, mysteriously different" from the other young women he knew.

Casimir fell in love with Manya, and she became enamored with him as well. Despite being the family governess, she knew the Zorawskis liked her. In fact, they treated her with great affection. It seemed as if there would be nothing to keep the young couple apart. Therefore, without apprehension, Casimir asked for his parents' approval for him and Manya to become engaged.

It didn't take long for Manya to find out her employers' true feelings. Monsieur Zorawski went into a rage! Madam Zorawski almost fainted. How could Casimir, their favorite child, even *consider* marrying a penniless governess who had to work for a living? It was a ridiculous notion. Moreover, he could have any girl in the neighborhood he wanted.

It must have seemed odd to Manya that no one considered the fact that Madam Zorawski had also worked as a governess at one point in her younger days. Nonetheless, Manya now knew where she ranked in the Zorawskis' estimation—they judged her as lacking in all the ways that counted. What did it matter that she was a good girl from an honorable family? That she was smart and cultivated or had a

spotless reputation? They considered her beneath them socially. Of course, Manya was hurt. She felt betrayed by her employers.

When Casimir, who was afraid of his parents' reproach and anger, reconsidered and did not push the matter any further, Manya "withdrew into awkward coldness and nervous silence." Again she felt betrayed. Casimir's true character, or rather lack of character, was a turning point. She decided right then that she would never again pursue love or a romantic relationship.

As humiliated as she must have felt, she did not leave her post with the Zorawskis, as she didn't want to worry her father or default on her commitment to help Bronya financially. She continued to give lessons and to study, but she was very unhappy. Life must have seemed cruel as she lost sight of love and of her dream to study in Paris. She began to focus all her hope on Bronya's and Jozio's futures, and remained dismayed with her own. She wrote to Jozio, "For now I have lost the hope of ever becoming anybody, all my ambition has been transferred to Bronya and you."

Still, Manya managed to find some positives and inner strength after her romantic disappointment. She wrote to Kazia, who had just announced her own engagement, "In spite of everything I came through it all honestly, with my head high." To her cousin Henrietta, she said, "Life does not deserve to be worried over," and later, "First principle: never let one's self be beaten down by persons or by events."

Moving On

THREE LONG years had passed since Manya had become a governess and Bronya had left to study at the Sorbonne in Paris. About this time, their father accepted a new directorship of a reform school not far from Warsaw. It was an unpleasant job, but the salary was high. He was able to send more money to Bronya, who immediately directed Manya not to send her any more financial support. Bronya asked her father to retain 8 rubles of the 40 he was now able to send her each month in order to start repaying Manya. From that moment on, Manya was able to start saving money.

Additionally, Bronya's letters brought the news of her successfully completed studies. She also revealed that she had fallen in love with a fellow Pole who lived in Paris, Casimir Dluski.

Thankfully, Manya's employment in Szczuki finally ended in early 1889, when the Zorawskis no longer needed her services. She was more than happy to make her way back to Warsaw and her father—at least until she departed for the Baltic coast to take another job, working for the Fuchs family. After spending some time at the Schultz Hotel during the summer, the Fuchs, their children, and Manya returned to Warsaw, where she spent the rest of the year in their employ as governess. Overall, the job went smoothly. But of course, anything would have been better than the humiliation she had suffered at the Zorawskis' home.

Manya continued to study, even as she worked for the Fuchs family, and she never lost her insatiable desire to learn. She still yearned for something more—but what? With her governess years almost behind her, Manya knew that she needed to figure out what direction to take next. She hoped that her future would soon become clearer.

PARIS AND PIERRE

3

One day a letter from Bronya arrived from Paris. In her quickly scribbled message, she explained that she and Casimir Dluski were planning to marry and she only needed to pass one last examination in order to be a doctor. She excitedly offered Manya the opportunity to come stay with her and Casimir in Paris for the coming year. She wrote, "And now you, my little Manya: you must make something of your life sometime. If you can get together a few hundred rubles this year you can come to Paris next year and live with us, where you will find board and lodging."

It is a sorrow to me to have to stay forever in Paris, but what am I to do? Fate has made us deeply attached to each other and we cannot endure the idea of separating.

—MARIE CURIE, IN A LETTER TO HER FRIEND KAZIA, CONCERNING HER ENGAGEMENT

Bronya must have been shocked by the reply. Manya used every excuse, from taking care of their father and Hela to urging Bronya to help Jozio instead, but the message was clear—she no longer wanted to go to Paris or study at the Sorbonne.

Bronya argued with Manya. She begged. She insisted. Nothing helped. Moreover, she was too poor to pay her younger sister's traveling expenses, so the matter was dropped—for the time being. Finally, it was decided that after finishing up her job as governess for the Fuchs, Manya would move back in with her father—who had just given up his own job— give lessons, and save up some money. *Then* she would consider going to Paris, although she was still not convinced she actually would.

Ready to Go at Last

THE EXTRA year that Manya spent in Warsaw turned out to be a pivotal one. The Flying University had opened its doors to her again, and she had access to a laboratory, located at 66 Krakovsky Boulevard. Manya's cousin directed the tiny building, which was deceptively called the Museum of Industry and Agriculture so as to not arouse Russian suspi-

Manya (standing) and Bronya (seated).
Musée Curie (coll. ACJC)

cion. It was here that Manya developed a taste for experimental research.

She worked in the lab as often as she could, sometimes coming home late at night. She experienced great joy and satisfaction in using **electrometers**, test tubes, and balances. Manya was in her element. Suddenly she felt a sense of purpose, a calling, and she was eager to follow it.

But despite her newly inflamed passion for science, and much to Bronya's dismay, Manya continued to put off setting a departure date to Paris. She gave Bronya many reasons for postponing. She wanted to help with Jozio's wedding. She was trying to assist Hela in finding a job. She needed to take care of their father. In reality, there may have been another reason for her stalling as well. Despite her disappointment in Casimir's reluctance to marry her against his parents' wishes, she was still in contact with him. Manya may have held out a glimmer of hope that the relationship might yet work out.

In September 1891, Manya was on holiday with friends at Zakopane in the Carpathians, and while there, she met up with Casimir. The two talked at length, and he still hesitated, refusing to go against his parents' wishes. That

The Sorbonne))

The Sorbonne is the name often used when referring to the historic University of Paris. However, the College of Sorbonne (founded in 1257) was actually just one school within the university, which had its origins in the 12th century. Located in a section of Paris known as the Latin Quarter, the university has always been considered one of the most prestigious schools in the world. In 1970 the University of Paris was split into 13 different universities, but all are still under a common chancellor.

The Sorbonne in Paris, France, 1890s. Author's collection

was it! Unable to bear it anymore, Manya told Casimir, "If you can't see a way to clear up our situation, it is not for me to teach it to you."

She was finally—and completely—done with the relationship. Her last barrier to going to Paris was gone. She didn't want to burden Bronya and her husband, but at last her decision was made. She was now ready to move on with her life and hopefully attend the Sorbonne. So, on September 23, 1891, she wrote to her sister, "Now, Bronya, I ask you for a definite answer. Decide if you can really take me in at your house, for I can come now."

As quickly as she could, Bronya happily responded with an affirmative answer, and Manya prepared for her journey. In advance, she sent everything she would need in Paris by freight. And because even a third-class ticket from Warsaw to Paris was too expensive, she procured a ticket on a fourth-class German railway carriage. It was a bare freight car, without compartments, and a bench on all four sides with an empty space in the middle where one could set up a folding chair.

So with "food and drink for three days on the train, the folding chair for the German carriage, books, a little bag of caramels, and a quilt," she was ready to go. As her father pulled her into his arms in a tender farewell on the boarding platform, she assured him that she would only be away for two or three years. Then she would return, and they would never be apart again. Little could she have known when she made her promise where this long-awaited journey would eventually take her.

Paris at Last: The "Heroic" Years

WHEN MANYA finally stepped off the train and breathed the air of a "free" country, she couldn't believe she was really in Paris. She could hardly contain her delight and excitement as she made her way toward Casimir and Bronya's modest home on Rue d'Allemagne. (*Rue* is the French word for street.) And later, as a horse-drawn bus carried her to the university, she took in everything—the Seine River, the towers of Notre Dame, and finally, the Sorbonne.

Yes, Manya had finally arrived. Although the Sorbonne's buildings had been under renovation for the last six years and the classrooms had to be rotated from one hall to another as the work progressed, the institution was still "the palace of her dreams." So with her small amount of money, Manya registered for classes and became a student in the Faculty of Science.

She chose to use the French style of her name, Marie, on her registration card. She may have arrived in Paris as Maria "Manya" Skłodowska, but from now on she would be known to those in Paris and at the Sorbonne as Marie Skłodowska, the quiet Polish girl who sat in the very front row of every class.

Marie ran into some problems right away. She thought she would be fluent enough in French to understand the Sorbonne's professors with no trouble. She had also assumed her self-directed scientific studies preparation from her governess days would be adequate for her to keep up with the class work in her math and physics courses. She was wrong.

She quickly discovered that she would have to put in an enormous amount of extra work in order to succeed in her classes. But hard work and determination had never been an issue for Marie. She was ecstatic to be a student at the Sorbonne, and she knew that she was finally where she was meant to be. It didn't take long for her to overcome her deficiencies and excel in her studies.

There were other challenges to Marie's academic life, though. Marie loved her sister. She was thankful for a place to stay. But she did not care for the constant interruptions to her study time, and the Dluskis loved to entertain friends often. Moreover, Marie's brother-in-law, Casimir, enjoyed amusements, music, concerts, political debates, and cultural experiences, and he and Bronya delighted in taking Marie with them to all their activities. In fact, at Casimir's insistence, Marie attended a special concert given by a starving Polish pianist, Ignace Paderewski, who would one day become the prime minister of a free Poland.

Ignace Jan Paderewski 𝄢

When Marie Curie listened to the concert given by the handsome, charismatic Polish pianist with wild, flowing red hair, she had no idea she was being entertained by the future prime minister of Poland. Of course, at that point any interruption to her study time was frustrating. But in years to come, Marie would appreciate not only this fiery-haired man's talent but also his shared passion and determination to work for a free Poland.

Paderewski was born on November 6, 1860, in a small village in southeastern Poland (now part of Ukraine). His mother died right after he was born, and when his father was arrested after the January Uprising of 1863, he was brought up by relatives. He showed early musical talent, and at the age of 12, he was admitted to the Warsaw

Marie heard Paderewski in concert long before he was famous.

Ignaz Jan Paderewski by Edward Algernon Baughan (Harvard Depository)

Conservatorium. Later he studied in Berlin and eventually made his musical debuts in Vienna in 1887 and Paris in 1890. He was also an instant success in the United States when he traveled there.

During World War I, he became an active member of the Polish National Committee in Paris, which was dedicated to reestablishing Poland as a free nation. Paderewski became the spokesperson for the organization and gained support from other world leaders. When World War I was over and Poland was once more a free nation, he became its first prime minister, in 1919.

Paderewski died on June 29, 1941. He is remembered today as a brilliant musician, composer, Polish patriot, leading statesman both before and after World War I, successful vineyard keeper, humanitarian, and friend to many prominent individuals of his day.

At the time, however, all the reveling was simply a nuisance. Marie needed quiet and solitude. In addition, Bronya and Casimir's home was quite a distance from the Sorbonne. It took Marie an hour by omnibus to reach the campus each day, which also meant two bus fares. Eventually she and the Dluskis decided that she should find inexpensive lodging near the school so that she would be able to walk to class each day.

She moved into a plain attic room in a middle-class house in the Latin Quarter neighborhood and somehow managed to live on only 40 rubles (around 100 francs) a month. There was no heat, lighting, or water in the room. There was only a tiny skylight and Marie's very few furnishings. She used an oil lamp, filled a pitcher with water at the tap on the landing, and cooked her simple meals on an alcohol heater. She also had a small coal heater. The room was uncomfortable at best, but it was quiet and close to the Sorbonne. For the next three years, she lived and studied in almost complete solitude.

Because her room was often cold, as she had to limit her coal use, Marie studied at the Sainte-Geneviève Library each evening until it closed at ten o'clock. Then she trudged home to her chilly quarters, lit her oil lamp, and continued studying until she fell into her small folding bed, exhausted, sometimes as late as two or three o'clock in the morning.

For weeks at a time, she might eat nothing but bread and tea, but Marie did not complain. Occasionally she had eggs or fruit, but her meager diet quickly resulted in malnutrition, weakness, and dizziness. She would often get so busy that she would forget to eat all day, and her sleep deprivation didn't help either.

Once she collapsed in front of one of her colleagues, who hurried to inform Bronya and Casimir, both physicians, about what had happened. Upset by Marie's poor health and lack of self-concern, Casimir immediately carried her to their home, where Bronya fed and cared for her younger sister for a few days while Marie regained her strength. However, as soon as Marie returned to her attic room, she continued on as before.

With no further thought about her living conditions, Marie happily attended classes in mathematics, chemistry, and physics and their accompanying labs. She gave herself up to nothing but school and study. The result was earning her long-coveted degree. Marie graduated at the top of her class in 1893 and received her degree in physics from the Sorbonne.

She thrived on gaining knowledge. It was her passion. And now that she'd had a taste of higher learning, she wanted even more. Marie desired to earn a second degree, this time in mathematics.

After graduating, her plan was to spend the summer in Poland with her father, then return to Paris in the fall to begin work on her mathematics degree. She gave up her attic room and stored her few possessions before leaving, but she also knew her savings were almost gone. She wasn't sure how she would get by when she returned to the Sorbonne, but she was determined to try. Fortunately, a friend of hers in Warsaw was able to help her secure a scholarship for Polish students with merit who wanted to study abroad. Marie would be awarded 600 rubles—enough to live on for over a year!

She was sad to leave her father again at summer's end but overjoyed to have the means to return to school. It also helped that she planned to return to Poland again after she earned her degree in mathematics. At that time, she would rejoin her father's household, find a teaching job, and remain in Poland permanently. At least, that was the plan.

Marie found another room to rent, on the sixth floor of a house on a good street near the Sorbonne. It was a great improvement over her last home, but she still had to watch her money carefully. However, her modest circumstances did not bother her in the least, even when she ran out of coal and was so cold she put on as many garments as she could and laid the rest on top of her covers to provide extra warmth as she tried to sleep. To her, the sacrifice was worth it.

Her brother-in-law Casimir later referred to this period in Marie's life as her "heroic years" because of all her suffering and self-sacrifice. However, she remembered them as a time of perseverance and accomplishment, despite her "sordid existence." She was proud of her independence and ability to make it as a single woman in a foreign country.

Enter Pierre Curie

IN 1894, while Marie was still in school, the Society for the Encouragement of National Industry hired her to perform a study on the magnetic properties of various steels. However, due to the cumbersome equipment required to complete the study, Marie needed somewhere other than a crowded laboratory to work.

She mentioned the problem to her Polish friend, Professor Jozef Kowalski, who was visiting the city with his young wife and giving lectures around Paris. Kowalski mentioned he had a friend who was a professor at the School of Physics and Chemistry on Rue Lhomond. Perhaps he could help Marie find a workroom, or at the very least, point her in the right direction.

Professor Kowalski invited Marie to tea with him and his wife the next evening. He also assured her that he would arrange for his professor friend to come as well so she could meet him. The young man's name was Pierre Curie.

After her disastrous relationship with Casimir Zorawski, Marie had sworn off love. Besides, she was single-minded in her quest for knowledge, passion for science, and loyalty to Poland. And there was also her father to consider, as she planned to return to her native country and move back in with him after graduation. So even though she was young and attractive, and had probably caught the attention of many a young man at the Sorbonne, Marie had no use for romance. She certainly did not go to the Kowalskis' for tea with the idea of finding a husband.

Incidentally, Pierre Curie felt the same way, and he had sworn off love and marriage as well. He'd even written in his journal years earlier, "Women, much more than men, love life for life's sake. Women of genius are rare."

Strong words about the opposite sex, for sure, but that was all about to change. Marie Skłodowska was definitely a woman of genius, as Pierre would soon discover.

Like Marie's Polish family, the Skłodowskis, the French Curies valued education and were forthright about what they believed in. Pierre Curie was born in Paris on May 15, 1859. His mother, Sophie-Claire Depouilly Curie, was the daughter of a prominent manufacturer of

When Marie met Pierre Curie, she was 26 and he was 35. Musée Curie (coll. ACJC)

Puteaux, near Paris. His father, Eugène, the son of a doctor, was a researcher and physician himself. Despite their standings, the Curies were never interested in society. They much preferred the quiet companionship of relatives and close friends and raising their family out in the country, away from the big city. Moreover, Dr. Curie was a free thinker and very outspoken in his political views.

Like their parents, Pierre and his older brother, Jacques, were highly intelligent and well educated. But it was evident early on that Pierre would not learn well in a traditional classroom. He was too dreamy and creative to sit at a desk all day. So Eugène allowed him to study at home and freely develop his love of natural science with excursions into the woods, where he would sometimes collect plants and animals for his father, who enjoyed studying nature.

This style of learning was perfect for Pierre! By the time he was 14—now under the tutelage of a remarkable professor named A. Bazille—he was extremely well prepared for higher learning. Professor Bazille, who taught Pierre math and physics and helped him catch up in Latin, immediately recognized the boy's genius. Due to his rapid progress, Pierre earned a bachelor

Brothers Jacques (back left) and Pierre (back right) Curie and their parents. Musée Curie (coll. ACJC)

Make Crystal Candy Sticks

PIERRE WAS A PIONEER in the field of **crystallography** and researcher in the role of **symmetry** in physics. You too can explore the formation of crystals by making your own rock-candy sticks.

Adult supervision required

You'll Need

* 3½–4 cups (700–800 g) granulated sugar
* 1½ cups (350 ml) water
* 2 wooden clothespins
* Food coloring (optional)
* 1 wooden skewer (cut in half and pointed ends removed)
* Plate
* Large pot
* 2 pint-sized (450-ml) glass jars

1. Soak the two wooden skewer halves in water and pour ½ cup (100 g) of the sugar onto a plate. Roll the skewers in the sugar so that half of each skewer is coated. Reserve the sugar for possible use later.

2. Attach a clothespin to the uncoated end of each skewer and set the skewers aside to dry.

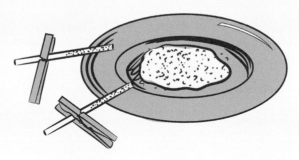

3. In a large pot, combine 3 cups (600 g) of sugar and the water. With an adult's supervision, bring the mixture to just a gentle boil. Then slowly add in more sugar, a little at a time, allowing it to dissolve each time, until no more will dissolve. Remove the pot from the heat. You can add a few drops of food coloring if you wish.

4. Carefully pour the sugar-water solution into the glass jars. Place each skewer into a jar, with the clothespin resting on the top of the jar. Make sure the skewers don't touch the bottoms or sides of the jars. Within three to four days, crystals of sugar will begin to form on the skewers. Leave the skewers in the jars until a thick layer of candy crystals develops around each stick.

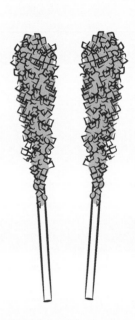

Note: If you want to make more candy sticks, you will need more skewers, sugar, and water. Just be sure to use a 2-to-1 ratio of sugar to water.

of science degree by age 16. By 18 he had the equivalent of a master's degree in physics.

Unfortunately, due to lack of money, Pierre did not immediately continue working on his doctorate at the Sorbonne, as he wished to do. At the age of 19, he secured a job as a laboratory assistant to Professor Paul Desains in the Faculty of Science. He held this position for five years, and it was during this time that he became interested in experimental research. Like Marie, a forced financial-related delay in schooling had actually led him to his life's work.

During this time, Pierre also worked with his brother, Jacques, with whom he had a very close relationship, to investigate the properties and symmetry of crystals. Jacques worked in one of the Sorbonne's mineralogy labs, so the two physicists were easily able to conduct experiments. It was a successful partnership, and the Curie brothers discovered a phenomenon called **piezoelectricity**. This effect happens when a certain kind of crystal is squeezed and an electric charge builds up on its surface. The discovery was exciting for other scientists, as they were finally able to measure small electric charges. And to go a step further, the Curie brothers also created a new scientific instrument, called a piezoelectric quartz electrometer, to precisely measure the tiny electric currents.

In 1883 Jacques was offered a professorship at the University of Montpellier in southeast France, and Pierre became chief of the laboratory at the School of Physics and Chemistry in Paris. The two would no longer be able to work or research together. However, in addition to teaching classes, Pierre continued studying crystalline physics on his own. This led to his formulation of the principle of symmetry: for any action on an object, the effect or result must have the same symmetry (balanced proportions) as its cause. The principle of symmetry is still very important in modern science.

Pierre also invented an ultrasensitive scientific scale called the Curie scale, which would be invaluable to Marie's research years later. Moreover, he studied **magnetism** and discovered "Curie's law," which explains how temperature affects magnetic fields.

By the time Marie met this brilliant, reserved physicist with rough beard, peaceful eyes, and deliberate speech, he was quite famous everywhere—except in his home country, that is. Although he had held his position at the School of Physics and Chemistry for 15 years, his salary was on the same level as that of a specialized factory worker.

For his part, however, Pierre had no interest in awards, medals, or promotions anyway. He simply loved science. And he had no desire to bother with anyone who would take him away from his first loves—his work and his laboratory. Besides, he thought, a woman in a laboratory would be a great distraction!

A Hesitant Marie

MARIE SAID of her first meeting with Pierre, at Professor Kowalski's home:

When I came in, Pierre Curie was standing in the window recess near a door leading to the balcony. He seemed very young to me, although he was then aged thirty-five. I was struck by the expression of his clear gaze and by a slight appearance of carelessness in his lofty stature. His rather slow, reflective words, his simplicity, and his smile, at once grave and young, inspired confidence. A conversation began between us and became friendly; its object was some questions of science upon which I was happy to ask his opinion.

Pierre was immediately smitten with the young Polish woman. Marie was intelligent as well as beautiful, and from that night on, he wanted to spend as much time with her as he possibly could. Besides their mutual love of science, their backgrounds were similar, so it wasn't too surprising when their friendship grew stronger in the spring of 1894.

Pierre was ready for their relationship to become more serious, but Marie was hesitant. When he suggested marriage in the early summer of 1894, she refused. She was studying for her second degree and intended to go back to Poland after her exams to visit family. She did

hope to return to France in the fall to work on a doctorate degree, but her plans were not definite. Her dream was still to teach and help those in Russia-controlled Poland have a better life.

She cared for Pierre with "great affection," but her loyalty to her family and Poland was strong. She felt that if she married this Frenchman, stayed in Paris, and became a French citizen, she would be turning her back on her country and her fellow Poles.

For his part, Pierre thought that he and Marie could do great things through science—they could make a difference in the world and for humankind. He wanted her to share his dream, but he also wanted her to share his life. He didn't give up easily. He pursued her through letters after she returned to her father's home in Warsaw. He desperately wanted her to come back to Paris in the fall, on any terms she chose.

Poor Pierre. She did give some encouragement by sending him a photo of herself though. And still he waited—and hoped. After spending the summer months in Poland Marie finally made the decision to return to Paris in October for one more year of study. She still would not accept Pierre's marriage proposal, but at least she was in the same country. And he kept trying to change her mind. He also took steps to present his **thesis** about the effect of heat on magnetic materials

Explore Magnetism: Make a Compass

WHEN MARIE MET PIERRE, she was research-ing the magnetic properties of steel. It's fitting, then, that when they set out on their honeymoon on bicycles, they carried a compass to help them navigate. Without magnetism, their compass would have been useless. In this activity, you will get to explore magnetism by making a hang-ing compass.

You'll Need
※ Magnet
※ Large steel sewing needle
※ Variety of small metal objects (paper clip, safety pin, screw, etc.)
※ String
※ Wooden skewer or pencil
※ Wide-mouthed glass jar
※ Standard compass (optional)

1. Carefully stroke the magnet down the full length of the large steel needle, from the eye to the point, 30–40 times. All strokes must go in the same direction.

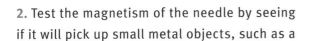

2. Test the magnetism of the needle by seeing if it will pick up small metal objects, such as a paper clip. If the needle isn't magnetized, stroke it with the magnet (in the same direction again) several more times.

3. Knot one end of the string to the eye of the needle. Adjust the knot if needed so that the needle dangles straight and level from the end of the string but does not touch the bottom of the jar.

4. Tie the other end of the string to the middle of the wooden skewer or pencil.

5. Lay the skewer or pencil across the top of the glass jar so the thread and needle are hanging down inside the jar without touching the bottom or sides. Shorten the string if necessary.

6. The needle in your homemade compass should automatically point to magnetic north. (You can compare the direction of your needle with the needle on a standard compass if you wish.)

Why Does This Happen?
Steel is made up of billions of tiny **atoms**, each having the property of a microscopic magnet. The atoms naturally group together in little blocks called domains, and the atoms in each domain point in the same direction. But the do-mains themselves are not necessarily lined up.

Envision billions of tiny bar magnets (domains) inside the needle going in different directions, cancelling out each other's magnetic ability.

When you rub the magnet along the needle in one direction, all the billions of domains become aligned, causing the needle to become magne-tized. This new magnetic field will then line up with the Earth's magnetic field.

to professors at the Sorbonne to complete the doctorate degree he had delayed for four years. Surely she could tell he meant business.

Even his mother, whom Marie's family met in early 1895, pulled Bronya aside and said, "There isn't a soul on earth to equal my Pierre. Don't let your sister hesitate. She will be happier with him than with anybody."

Finally, to show her just how serious he was about her, Pierre offered to move to Poland, if only she would accept his hand in marriage.

He could teach French and do research and experiments there just as well.

At this, after almost a year of saying no, Marie agreed to marry Pierre and stay in France. However, they planned to visit Poland the next year.

Upon hearing of the engagement, her brother, Jozio, wrote to her, "I think you are right to follow your heart, and no just person can reproach you for it." Her father approved of the match as well. Marie was satisfied.

Bicycles: All the Rage! 🎵

When Marie and Pierre married in 1895, bicycles were no longer viewed as dangerous toys for daredevil boys, as they had been in the past. In fact, the development of the "safety" bicycle in the 1880s changed bicycle history, with the machines now regarded as a safe and practical means of getting around for both men and women.

Bicycles were at their height of popularity in the 1890s, when there was a boom in bike production and use. They were the rage in both the United States and Europe. The safety bicycles had two equal-sized small wheels, a chain driver, gears, and brakes. While some people still considered it improper for females to ride, bicycles now allowed women more movement from place to place, which led to greater freedom and independence, both in travel and in fashion. Although Marie shortened her own skirts only a bit to be able to pedal and walk freely, many women felt their cycling hobby called for more sensible fashion. Long, heavy skirts that reached down to the ankles, causing a safety hazard, were soon replaced by either shorter skirts or bloomers. This new "bicycle costume" was just the beginning of a major change in women's fashion during the coming years.

A New Life Together

BRONYA'S MOTHER-IN-LAW offered to make Marie's wedding dress, and no-nonsense Marie asked that it be practical and dark so she could later wear it to work in the lab! And with the same lack of fanfare, Marie and Pierre were wed on July 26, 1895. That morning they rode the train to Sceaux, where Pierre's parents lived. A judge performed the ceremony at city hall. Then they returned to the elder Curies' home for a small reception with close friends and family.

Using wedding gift money, Marie purchased two bicycles. After the reception, she and Pierre pedaled off through the rolling hills of the French countryside for the honeymoon they affectionately called their "wedding tramp." They enjoyed peaceful days exploring nature, picnicking in woodland glades, and staying in country inns. It was a happy time for the newlyweds.

Pierre and Marie pedaled away to spend their honeymoon in the French countryside.
Musée Curie (coll. ACJC)

NEW DISCOVERIES!

After their honeymoon, Marie and Pierre returned to Paris in October. They set up housekeeping in a small flat at 24 Rue de la Glacière, not far from Pierre's work. Because they had no plans to entertain guests, they turned down offers of furniture from Pierre's parents. Two chairs were just right—one for him and one for her. No need to encourage visitors to sit and stay!

We had an especial joy in observing that our products containing concentrated radium were all spontaneously luminous.

—MARIE CURIE

Marie was determined to keep their home as simple as possible, as she was busy working and didn't want to spend time on needless cleaning. But she did take her role as Pierre's wife very seriously and kept up with their expenses carefully. With only 500 francs per month coming in from Pierre's work until she earned the diploma that would allow her to teach in France, Marie knew she had to help make ends meet. Of course, being economical was nothing new for her! However, working for long hours at the lab on top of running a household *was* tiring. She also made it a point of honor to learn basic cooking skills from Bronya's mother-in-law. Marie was as detailed with the notes in her cookbooks as she was with her work in the lab.

Pierre and Marie were well suited because they both wanted to focus only on science and each other. He continued teaching and studying the structure of crystals, and she kept up her research on the magnetic properties of steel. She was even allowed to share Pierre's workspace at the School of Physics and Chemistry. She also used the time to prepare for and place first in a fellowship examination that would give her certification to teach high school physics. Life was busy and full, and almost a year and a half had slipped by when

Pierre in the lab. Musée Curie (coll. ACJC)

Marie found out she was expecting their first child.

The Curies' daughter Irène was born on September 12, 1897, and delivered by her grandfather Eugène Curie. Though she now had a new baby at home, Marie never considered giving up her work. She planned to balance her roles and do them all equally well. According to legend, even when she was extremely busy with her research and work, Marie never once missed giving her baby her nightly bath.

As her younger daughter, Ève, wrote years later, "She was resolved to face love, maternity, and science, all three, and to cheat none of them. By passion and will she was to succeed."

Shortly after Irène was born, Pierre's mother died from cancer. His father, wanting to be closer to his grandchild, agreed to move in with Marie and Pierre. This turned out to be a good arrangement for everyone. With their daughter in good hands, the couple agreed it was time for Marie to get back on track earning her doctorate degree.

At that time, no other European woman had ever achieved such a high degree in physics. This would be another first for the young physicist. However, before Marie could progress, she had to decide on a subject on which she could write her doctoral thesis. With so many exciting things happening in the world of science in the late 1800s, what would she choose?

The X-Ray

WHILE MARIE and Pierre had been setting up their first home and starting a family, scientists were making discoveries at a rapid pace. In November of 1895, German physicist Wilhelm Röntgen accidentally discovered a new kind of ray, which he called an X-ray—the X meaning it was unknown.

Röntgen had been studying chemicals that glowed when they were exposed to light. While he was holding a special kind of tube called a

Wilhelm Röntgen discovered the X-ray.
Author's collection

cathode-ray tube (also called a Crookes tube, named after its inventor), he noticed that a special **fluorescent**-painted screen across the room glowed when the cathode-ray tube was on. Puzzled, he covered the tube with light-blocking paper. The screen still glowed! What were these strange rays?

On a whim, he put his hand between the tube and the screen. He was totally shocked by what he saw on the screen. It was an image of the bones in his hand! The mysterious rays passed right through his skin and flesh, and only his bones left a shadow. Because the rays also exposed photographic plates, he was able to capture a picture for evidence.

One of the most famous X-rays of all time is the skeleton of Röntgen's wife's hand, which clearly shows the wedding ring on her finger. With the publication of his findings at the end of 1895, Röntgen's X-rays caused quite a stir around the world, especially among doctors. Röntgen truly believed his findings would help people, so he did not patent X-rays or try to make money from his discovery. He later died penniless.

Mysterious New Rays

NOT LONG after Röntgen presented his findings, a French physicist discovered yet another unknown ray. Henri Becquerel, who came from a long line of scientists, was doing his own experiments with X-rays and **uranium**, an **element** that had been discovered in 1789 and named for the planet Uranus.

Becquerel knew that certain materials gave off a **phosphorescent** glow after being exposed to direct light. He wanted to find out if these phosphorescent materials also gave off X-rays. He put some uranium **compound** samples in the sun; then while they were still glowing, he put them on top of a photographic plate that had been covered in dark paper. When he developed the plate, he found the imprint of the samples. He concluded that the rays were indeed able to pass through paper.

Next, he wanted to find out if the rays could go through copper. He put a copper cross on top of another wrapped photographic plate, and was about to put a uranium sample in the sun to expose it to direct light when it started to rain. He set the sample on top of the cross on the photographic plate and put it in a drawer to use another day. Several cloudy, rainy days followed.

Frustrated by the weather, Becquerel decided to develop the plate anyway. He was astonished. The imprint of the copper cross could clearly be seen on the photographic plate, but the uranium sample had not been "excited" by the sun at all. In fact, the impression was even clearer than the ones made with uranium samples that *had* been exposed to the sun. The rays had emitted spontaneously.

Henri Becquerel, 1904.

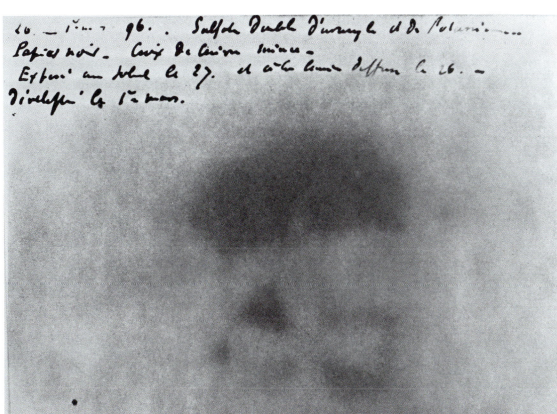

If you look closely, you can see the imprint of the Maltese cross caused by spontaneous radiation on this photographic plate that Becquerel developed on March 1, 1896. Musée Curie (coll. ACJC)

Upon further research, Becquerel concluded that all minerals containing uranium could continue to give off mysterious rays for years without weakening. These rays could go through most objects, reflect and bend like light through a **prism**, and even give off a weak electric current. Fascinating!

Becquerel wrote six papers about his research in 1897, then moved on to other subjects. His findings did not stir up the same excitement as Röntgen's. Moreover, he assumed there was nothing else to discover about the subject, and no other scientists seemed inclined to pick up where he left off. The origin and nature of the **radiation** remained a mystery, and the field was wide open for anyone interested in digging deeper.

Marie was definitely interested!

Make Sun Prints

MARIE'S DECISION TO RESEARCH X-rays and **radioactivity** for her doctoral thesis stemmed from Henri Becquerel's discovery of **spontaneous radiation** while working with uranium. Becquerel thought he needed the sun to "excite" his phosphorescent samples in order for them to give off X-rays and make an impression on a photographic plate. Of course, it turned out that the radium samples spontaneously produced radiation without help from the sun.

However, for a fun project, *you* can use the sun's rays to make interesting prints on construction paper.

You'll Need
※ Black construction paper
※ Several objects you want to make a print of (leaves, keys, scissors, etc.)
※ Clear or masking tape (optional)

1. Place a sheet of black construction paper on a flat surface in a sunny spot outdoors. It's important for the paper to get full sun.

2. Lay different objects on top of the paper. You can create a collage or use a single object with an interesting shape. For example, fern leaves make a nice presentation. If you are worried about your objects moving or blowing away, secure them underneath with small pieces of tape.

3. Leave the construction paper and objects in the sun for several hours. Then remove the objects from the top of the paper to see the prints left behind.

What Happened?
The solar UV rays broke down the chemical bonds in the paper and caused fading—sort of a bleaching effect. Only the areas where the objects blocked the sun remained unchanged, leaving a cool negative print.

The Research Shed

BOTH MARIE and Pierre were fascinated by Becquerel's research. Where did the tiny bit of energy in the uranium compounds come from? What was its nature? Marie thought these were questions that a doctoral thesis and research could be based upon. She had to be very careful with her decision because it was possible to spend years researching a subject only to find it was a dead end. But in the end, Marie was sure that the study of uranium rays was the right choice.

There remained one problem, however. Where could Marie do her research and experiments? She had no lab of her own, so Pierre asked the director of the School of Physics and Chemistry for a place. The only available space was an old glassed-in studio on the ground floor of the school at Rue Lhomond. At one time it had been used for storage, and it was not a comfortable workspace in the least. The room was damp and cold, and in the winter, the temperature could drop as low as 44 degrees Fahrenheit (about 7 degrees Celsius)! The conditions were certainly not the best for Marie's health or the precise, scientific instruments she needed to use, but she was undaunted.

While Marie began her work to explore uranium's rays and radiation, Pierre continued his work with crystals. And as it turned out, the piezoelectric quartz electrometer that he and Jacques had developed in their early partnership was just what Marie needed for her experiments. The brothers had discovered that when the quartz crystal at the top of their electrometer was squeezed, an electrical charge built up on its surface. This piezoelectric effect allowed scientists to measure tiny amounts of electricity in the air given off by other samples by comparing it to the known amount of charge given off by the quartz crystal.

Marie would use the electrometer to determine the strength of uranium's rays by measuring the small electric charge each sample gave off into the air surrounding it. Easier said than done! The electrometer was so delicate that even a fingerprint could change a reading. It took Marie three weeks to master the instrument.

She began measuring the strength of the rays in different amounts of uranium. She discovered that the larger the size a uranium sample was, the stronger the rays were: so bigger samples emitted more radiation. Other factors, such as temperature, didn't seem to matter. It obviously came down to the number of atoms present in each sample.

Then Marie began to wonder if other elements besides uranium also gave off these strange rays. The only way to find out was to test all the known elements. At the time she began her research, there were only 79 known chemical elements on the periodic table developed by Dmitri Mendeleev, and Marie planned to experiment with each one. She eventually discovered that the element thorium gave off a weaker form of radiation.

That uranium and thorium could spontaneously produce radiation was a new idea. There wasn't even a word for this marvelous occurrence yet, so Marie created one. She called the phenomenon **radioactivity**, and the affected elements **radio elements**. She also correctly reasoned that radioactivity existed due to something happening within the element's atoms—or atomic activity. Simply put, the rays were a property of the atoms inside the elements. This was a huge discovery, but Marie was far from completing her research. So after making a report of her findings to the French Academy of Sciences in April 1898, she got right back to work.

The Element Is There and I've Got to Find It

SINCE SHE had already tested all known elements for Becquerel's rays, Marie decided to focus on compound minerals containing at least some uranium or thorium. If she found any radioactivity in the sample, she explored further. Inexplicably, some of the samples emitted levels of radiation that were much higher than they should have been based on the amount of uranium or thorium they held.

Marie became especially intrigued with ore of uranium, or **pitchblende**, a naturally occurring, heavy black mineral from which uranium is extracted. It also contains thorium. But amazingly, pitchblende showed a degree of radioactivity four times greater than the uranium (or thorium) that could have been extracted from the sample. Something was not adding up!

At first Marie assumed she had made a mistake with her measurements, but after testing and retesting the samples repeatedly, the results stayed the same. She reasoned that it could only mean one thing—she had discovered the presence of a new element!

Soon after, she said to Bronya, "You know, Bronya, the radiation that I couldn't explain comes from a new chemical element. The element is there and I've got to find it. We are sure! The physicists we have spoken to believe we have made an error in experiment and advise us to be careful. But I am convinced that I am not mistaken."

Knowing that other scientists were right behind her with their research and discoveries, Marie wanted to go ahead and write a scientific paper about her findings. On April 12, 1898, the first communication was presented to the French Academy of Sciences by Professor Gabriel Lippmann and published in its weekly

Mendeleev and the Periodic Table))

Dmitri Ivanovich Mendeleev was a Russian chemist who drew up the first periodic table of elements. He began arranging the known elements (60 at the time) into rows of increasing **atomic weight**, starting with the lightest, **hydrogen** (which became **atomic number** 1), up to the heaviest. Atomic weight is the mass of one atom of an element. Atomic number is the number of protons in the nucleus of an atom. Atomic number also determines where an element is located on the periodic table.

If Mendeleev came to an element that behaved like one with a lower atomic weight, he would start a new row and drop that element right under the earlier one that had similar behavior or characteristics. By doing this, he observed that the vertical columns now formed a family of elements with common behaviors.

Mendeleev was so sure he was on the right track that if the next element's atomic weight didn't follow the ascending pattern, he skipped a space, figuring there was a missing element yet to be discovered. As each new element was found, Mendeleev revised his table. By the time Marie started her research, there were 79 known chemical elements.

Today there are 92 known naturally occurring elements, as well as many artificial ones, on Mendeleev's periodic table of elements. The elements can be divided into metals and non-metals, but these two groups are very large. Therefore, the metals are further divided into three more groups: alkali, transition, and inner transition. All elements with atomic numbers greater than 83 are radioactive.

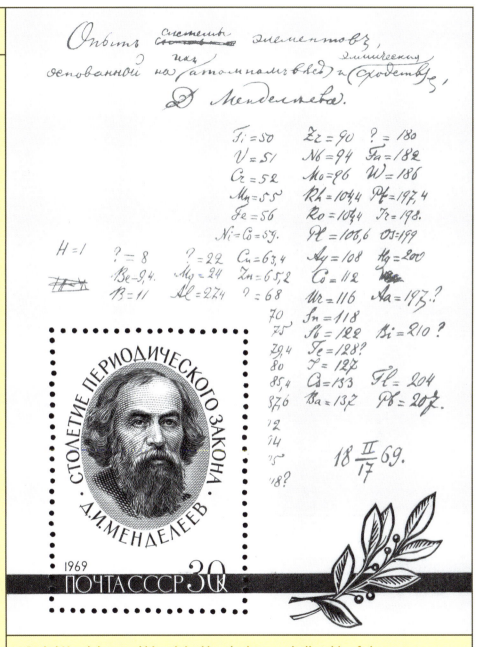

Dmitri Mendeleev and his original handwritten periodic table of elements.
USSR postal stamp, June 20, 1969, CPA 3762, sheet of 1

Marie and Pierre working together in their lab.
Author's collection

journal, *Proceedings*: "Marie Skłodowska Curie announced the probable presence in pitchblende ores of a new element endowed with powerful radioactivity."

As she probably expected, there was no sudden hoopla. Marie knew she would have to isolate the element even further to determine atomic weight and its unique light pattern in order to satisfy skeptics and make her findings official. The work was far from over.

Because Pierre was so fascinated by Marie's discovery and wanted to help her stay ahead of the scientific pack, he put aside his own work on crystals and joined her. Together they determined to isolate the new element that Marie was certain she had found in the pitchblende.

Marie and Pierre set about separating all the individual elements in the pitchblende, using chemicals and a process they developed themselves. Afterward they took out the known components and focused on the unknown ones. They kept meticulous notes about the process in notebooks that contained entries in both their handwritings—Marie's on the right-hand pages and Pierre's on the left.

They started by working with one small batch of pitchblende at a time, boiling each in an **alkali** solution. After the water had boiled away, they collected the salty-looking residue and processed it further. With each step, the substance became more solid, as well as more radioactive.

By June 1898, the Curies had figured out that two separate batches of the pitchblende residue became radioactive at different points. One batch seemed to be associated with the element bismuth, and the other batch with the element barium, neither of which was radioactive on its own. The longer they tested, the more convinced Marie and Pierre became that they had discovered not just one new element but two!

A New Element: Polonium

BY THE time Marie began her research, much had already been discovered about elements. She knew that when an element is heated to a certain point, it glows. The light it gives off can be studied through a prism, and each element's light produces its own unique pattern, called spectral lines. She also knew that eight other elements had been identified and proven by their special spectral lines. Perhaps she could use this science of **spectroscopy** to prove the existence of her new elements as well.

The Curies called upon Eugène-Anatole Demarçay, a French expert and colleague in the field of spectroscopy, to see if he could help them identify in their sample any unique spectral lines that were associated with bismuth. Alas, none appeared at that point.

However, Marie figured they just needed to purify the substance even more. It was back to work. She met with Eugène-Anatole again on July 18, 1898, with a more purified sample to find out if he could detect anything. When he put the sample into his spectroscope, a colored line appeared—one he had never seen before. At last! Marie finally had proof that she had indeed discovered a new element. When Pierre asked her what she wanted to call her new element, she decided on **polonium**, in honor of her beloved Poland.

The Curies were thrilled to make a formal announcement about their discovery of polonium in the French Academy of Sciences' *Proceedings*: "We believe the substance we have extracted from pitchblende contains a metal not yet observed, related to bismuth by its analytical properties. If the existence of this new metal is confirmed we propose to call it polonium, from the original country of one of us."

However, because extracting enough polonium to determine its atomic weight was too difficult, Marie decided to put it aside in order to focus on the "other" element. But first, she and Pierre took a much-needed three-month vacation with their little daughter, away from the noisy, hot city. Oddly, Pierre was suffering pains in his legs, which he thought were caused by rheumatism, and Marie's fingertips boasted sores. Perhaps in this rented country house in the small village of Auroux, they could rest, relax, and recuperate.

A New Element: Radium

It was not long after the Curies returned to Paris that Bronya and her family moved back to Poland to open a treatment center for tuberculosis patients. Marie was sad and desperately missed her sister, but she knew her work had to go on.

With her usual determination, Marie was ready to tackle the job of separating out her other new element from the batch of pitchblende associated with barium. She and Pierre used the same process they had used to purify polonium, and what they discovered was astounding. The sample was 900 times more radioactive than uranium! When tested with the spectroscope, it too produced its own unique spectral lines. Marie had proof that she had indeed found a second previously unknown element. She decided to call it **radium**.

On December 26, 1898, the Academy of Sciences published the Curies' announcement and findings in a paper titled "On a New, Strongly Radioactive Substance Contained in Pitchblende."

The paper detailed the Curies' experiments and results. It concluded with, "The new radioactive substance contains a new element to which we propose to give the name of RADIUM.

The new radioactive substance certainly contains a very strong proportion of barium; in spite of that its radioactivity is considerable. The radioactivity of radium therefore must be enormous."

New Challenges and a New Lab

MARIE HAD announced the existence of two new elements. She had also upset the previously accepted scientific ideas on the composition of matter. But nobody had actually seen the radium in its purest form, and some were still skeptical. Most chemists want to "see" a substance, weigh it, and examine it before being 100 percent convinced of its existence. So to further prove herself, Marie needed to isolate enough pure radium from the pitchblende to establish its atomic weight (the average weight of an atom within an element). This was not going to be easy, because radium only existed in trace amounts. And two big problems immediately presented themselves.

First, the Curies needed a very large amount of pitchblende—at least a ton. Because of uranium's commercial value, pitchblende was expensive. However, Marie and Pierre found out that the Austrian government had a uranium mine and was willing to let them buy, at a reasonable price, several tons of the residue left over after the uranium

had been extracted. They could use this as their primary material.

The second problem was that, because they would be processing such a large amount of pitchblende, Marie's closet-sized storage shed wouldn't be big enough to work in. Once again, Pierre approached his boss. The only place available this time was another empty shed that medical students had used in the past as a dissection lab where they kept cadavers. Not ideal by any means. But at least it was right across from Marie's workroom turned lab. They would have access to both sheds and the courtyard in between.

Because Pierre was the more experienced lab researcher, they decided that Marie would extract and purify, and he would do the calculations and study the physical properties of radium.

It was no surprise that the work was grueling and backbreaking. Marie started with large 44-pound batches of pitchblende and boiled each in different solutions in large vats to try to separate the radium and barium. The fumes were noxious and the shed had no ventilation, so she often worked in the courtyard. This meant that on rainy days, she would have to drag the heavy containers back inside. For hours at a time, she stirred the liquids and transferred batches from one vat of solution to another. Each time the water boiled away, it left a residue, which Marie would rinse and

Marie and Pierre dubbed their workspace the Shed of Discovery. Musée Curie (coll. ACJC)

treat to refine even further. Finally, she was left with **radium salt**.

Next, she used a type of fractional crystallization to separate other substances from the radium salt. This proved tricky because of the constant presence of iron and coal dust inside the old shed. Still, she pushed ahead with grit and determination for the next four years. Initially Marie thought that radium made up around 1 percent of the pitchblende. Would she have persevered if she had known it was actually one millionth of 1 percent? Knowing Marie, probably so!

She would later write of that time, "In spite of the difficulties of our working conditions, we felt very happy. In our poor shed there reigned a great tranquility." She also noted, "We lived in our single preoccupation as if in a dream."

Finding Extra Income

As their work with radium progressed, the Curies were spending a good bit of their own money on the research. Plus they had moved out of their flat and into a house. Even with Pierre's regular job at the School of Physics and Chemistry, finances were tighter than usual. They had even turned down good-paying positions at the University of Geneva, Switzerland, because packing up and moving would have taken too much time away from Marie's research. With that refusal, they also turned down the chance to have their own real, professionally equipped laboratory. But time was of the essence—and they didn't have any to spare if they wanted to stay ahead of the game.

A physicist friend of theirs, Henri Poincaré, was able to help Pierre get an additional teaching job at the Sorbonne. Between working at two different schools and helping Marie, he was very busy. Marie was also able to secure a job teaching physics at the Higher Normal School for Girls in nearby Sèvres. The extra income was welcome and certainly eased their financial situation, but the time away from the work shed must have been frustrating to both Curies. Moreover, Marie put a lot of energy into being a good mother to Irène. She quickly lost 15 pounds keeping up such a frantic pace at work and at home!

Around this time, Marie also hired a much-needed lab assistant named André-Louis Debierne. In 1899, while working for the Curies, he independently discovered the element actinium when he separated it from the pitchblende residues left after the Curies had finished extracting the radium. Debierne would prove to be an invaluable helper and friend for the next 35 years.

The Secret to Success

In between her other responsibilities of teaching and caring for her family, Marie

Make Elephant Toothpaste

WHEN MARIE DID EXPERIMENTS for her research, she did not always know in advance what the reaction would be. You, too, can learn about reactions when you make "elephant toothpaste" by adding yeast to a hydrogen peroxide and soap solution. Be warned, however: this experiment can get messy. But it will also be very fun!

Adult supervision required

You'll Need
* Safety glasses
* 2-liter plastic soda bottle (label removed)
* Foil baking pan
* Funnel
* 1 cup (240 ml) 3% hydrogen peroxide (H_2O_2)
* Dish soap
* Food coloring
* 1 tablespoon (8 g) active dry yeast
* 3 tablespoons (45 ml) warm water
* Sugar (optional)
* Small bowl

1. Put on your safety glasses. Stand the plastic soda bottle in the center of the foil baking pan. Using the funnel, pour

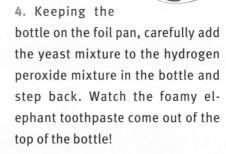

the hydrogen peroxide into the bottle.

2. Add a couple of squirts of dish soap and several drops of food coloring to the hydrogen peroxide and swirl it around to combine. Set aside.

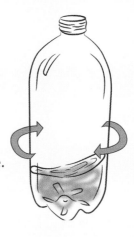

3. Add the active dry yeast to the warm water in a small bowl and stir until dissolved. Adding a pinch of sugar to the yeast mixture may speed up the fermentation process. Let the mixture sit for three minutes until all the yeast is dissolved.

4. Keeping the bottle on the foil pan, carefully add the yeast mixture to the hydrogen peroxide mixture in the bottle and step back. Watch the foamy elephant toothpaste come out of the top of the bottle!

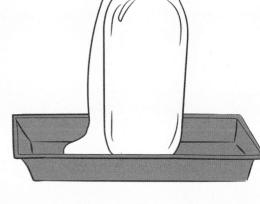

What Happened?
The yeast contains an enzyme called catalase, which acts as a **catalyst** to help break down and remove the oxygen from the hydrogen peroxide. The resulting oxygen gas gets trapped in the soap, which causes foam to pour out of the top of the bottle.

continued trying to isolate enough radium to see and measure. It must have seemed like an endless process—steps to repeat thousands of times. Dissolving. Crystallizing. Redissolving. Recrystallizing. Over and over. She wondered

to her husband, "I wonder what It will be like, what It will look like."

"I don't know," Pierre replied. "I should like it to have a very beautiful color."

She persisted slowly and methodically, and with each action, the radium salt became more pure—and more radioactive.

One night, after tucking Irène into bed and leaving her under the watchful eye of her grandfather Eugène, Marie and Pierre made their way to their Shed of Discovery, as they called it. When they entered the shed that winter evening in 1901, a breathtaking sight met their eyes. The tiny dishes of radium salts, each at different stages of the purification process, gave off a strange but **luminous** and beautiful bluish light. Marie and Pierre stood quietly in the dark room and simply basked in the glow of all their hard work.

Marie had finally isolated a tiny bit of pure radium salt, one-tenth of a gram—about the size of a grain of rice. But it was enough! Later Marie would say of her success, "The secret is in not going too fast." After four long years of backbreaking work, she could finally prove to all scientists and humankind that radium *did* exist.

Marie wasted no time in writing and publishing papers about radium and radioactivity. Her first measurement of radium's atomic weight was noted as 225.93, which wasn't exactly right, but it was extremely close to the current agreed value of 226. (The precise atomic weight of a radium atom is actually 226.0254.) Nevertheless, before long, information about the Curies and their radium research spread like wildfire. Scientists all over the world took notice and became interested in the study of radium and what it could mean to the world of science.

At last, her element, radium, had earned its place on Mendeleev's periodic table. It was put right below barium in the column for alkaline earth metals.

The Curies' success was not without its drawbacks, however. They still suffered from health problems brought on, they thought, by exhaustion. Even so, at the public confirmation of her discovery, Marie was ecstatic! Yet, this most rewarding phase of her life would soon be followed by one of the most turbulent.

KONGLIGA SVENSKA
VETENSKAPS-AKADEMIEN

har vid sitt sammanträde den 12 Nov.
1903, i enlighet med föreskrifterna i det af

ALFRED NOBEL

den 27 November 1895 upprättade testa-
mente, beslutat att tilldela hälften af det pris
som detta år bortgifves åt den som inom
fysikens område har gjort den viktigaste
upptäckt eller uppfinning till

PIERRE CURIE

OCH HANS HUSTRU FRU

MARIE CURIE

såsom ett erkännande af den utomordentliga
förtjenst de inlagt genom sina gemensamt

utfö
He
fer

FAME WITH A SIDE OF TROUBLE

As you have seen, fortune favors us at this moment; but these favors of fortune do not come without many worries. We have never been less tranquil than at this moment. There are days when we scarcely have time to breathe.

—PIERRE CURIE, IN A 1902 LETTER TO E. GOUY

Not long after Marie wrote the atomic weight for radium in her lab notebook and set the scientific world on its ear, she received some very sad news from her family in Poland. Her father was seriously ill due to complications from a gallbladder operation. Marie immediately boarded a train to hurry to his side. Sadly, he passed away before she could arrive.

Marie, now 35, took her father's death hard. He had been her mentor, her friend, and one of her biggest supporters. When her mother had died, he'd been there for his daughter—always. She was heartbroken that she had not been able to see her father one last time. She also believed that she had disappointed him by not returning to Poland as originally planned. At his coffin, she begged his forgiveness.

Of course, she was needlessly torturing herself with such thoughts. Vladislav had been extremely proud of his "Anciupecio" (her family's special nickname for her since she was a baby) and her accomplishments. His greatest joys in his later years had come from following Marie's work. However, when Marie returned to Paris, her happiness was still greatly dimmed.

At the dawn of the 1900s, around the same time that Marie was beginning to gain a great deal of attention in the scientific world, several other hardships befell her and her family. She had been expecting another child, but the baby girl died shortly after birth. Then she found out that Bronya's second child, a little boy, had died of meningitis.

Marie's health continued to decline, and she was always fatigued. She even suffered from a condition called somnambulism, which often caused her to sleepwalk through the house at night. Despite her own ailments, she was more concerned about Pierre, who continued to regularly suffer violent attacks of pain. However, only once did she hear him complain, "It's pretty hard, this life that we have chosen."

Despite their amazing discovery and the satisfaction it brought, Marie became frightened.

What was wrong with Pierre? Did he have some dreadful disease? What if something happened to her husband? She asked him, "Pierre... if one of us disappeared... the other should not survive.... We can't exist without each other, can we?

He firmly replied, "You are wrong. Whatever happens, even if one has to go on like a body without a soul, one must work just the same."

In this very trying time, he wanted to remind her of their common mission, and in his mind, a scientist had no right to desert science, the object of his life!

So Marie and Pierre continued on as before and published (either together, separately, or collaboratively with their colleagues) 32 reports about their work and on the subjects of radium and radioactivity. With such a wealth of information being distributed among the scientific community, more and more people became interested in the Curies' research and findings, which the couple shared freely.

The Study of Radioactivity

WHEN MARIE first began her research, scientists believed that elemental atoms always stayed the same—never changing. However, when the Curies discovered the phenomenon of radioactivity, that belief was challenged in a very big way. Obviously, atoms of elements *did* change! Many other scientists jumped on the radioactivity bandwagon to see what they might discover.

Two such scientists were Ernest Rutherford and Frederick Soddy, colleagues and friends of the Curies. A young physicist from New Zealand, Ernest Rutherford first worked with J. J. Thompson, the British physicist who in 1897 discovered electrons—the first subatomic particle to be identified. Then after hearing about Henri Becquerel's work with uranium, Rutherford decided to explore its radioactivity. He discovered that a radioactive ray from uranium could be split into two parts using a magnet. The two parts differed in their ability to penetrate different materials.

He called the part of the ray that was the weakest an alpha ray. It was slower and heavier and could be deflected by something as simple as a sheet of thin metal foil. He called the other a beta ray. It was faster, could be easily bent by the positive pole of the magnet, and penetrated barriers 100 times thicker than was possible for the alpha ray. (Later, a third ray, called a gamma ray, would be discovered. It was the strongest and could penetrate very thick materials.) Scientists would use this information to understand atomic structure.

Rutherford also discovered the concept of a **half-life**, which means how long it takes for one-half of the atoms in an unstable element to go through a decay process to release en-

ergy (radioactivity) and transform into the atoms of a completely different element. This decay also produces alpha, beta, and gamma radiation.

Frederick Soddy, an English radiochemist, helped Rutherford demonstrate these findings. Then, working with Sir William Ramsay in 1903, Soddy discovered that the decay of radium produces helium gas. Later, he was also able to confirm that uranium did indeed decay into radium. This work showed that a radioactive element may have more than one **atomic mass**, though the chemical properties are identical. Soddy and his assistant, Ada Hitchins, called these different atomic masses of the same element **isotopes** (a name suggested by Dr. Margaret Todd).

The idea of atoms changing within elements and the resulting radioactivity might have caught the interest of the scientific community, but the rest of the world was more fascinated by the effect of radium on human flesh!

Other scientists had reported red blisters and burns on the skin when it was exposed to radium salts, so Pierre decided to find out for himself. He put some radium salt on his arm for 10 hours to see what happened. Big mistake! He suffered a terrible burn, and the resulting lesion took four months to heal. He wrote a report to the Academy of Sciences detailing his burn, its healing process, and the

Ernest Rutherford. Library of Congress Prints and Photographs Division, George Grantham Bain Collection (LC-DIG-ggbain-03392)

fact that Marie's fingertips were burned and permanently scarred from handling radium. Henri Becquerel also experienced a burn similar to Pierre's (though not intentional) when he carried a vial of radium salts in his pocket. He too wrote an article.

Medical professionals who read these reports began to question and wonder: If radium caused the death of human tissue, might it also destroy cancer? Pierre and Marie provided samples of radium to doctors so they could try out the treatment (which became known as **curietherapy**) on patients with cancer. Many treatments were very successful, and with such positive results, a radium industry was born!

Recognition and Reward

IN EARLY 1903, the Curies received a letter from the United States. Because of various researchers' success in using radium to treat malignant tumors, some technicians were asking for information on how to isolate and produce it. They wanted to duplicate the process Marie had invented and perfected. Pierre and Marie discussed their options. They could detail the full process and give away the information freely—or they could patent the process and assure themselves of all rights.

The Curies could have gotten extremely rich by patenting their extraction process, as anyone using it would have had to pay them. Their financial woes would have ended immediately. They could have had their own state-of-the-art laboratory.

Half-Life 🌒

When the Curies discovered polonium and radium, scientists believed that atoms of elements never changed. In 1913, Frederick Soddy proposed the idea of isotopes—alternate versions of the same element with the same chemical properties but different atomic weights. The number of protons in each atom is the same, but the number of neutrons isn't. Isotopes are like siblings from the same family.

Some isotopes are stable. Some are unstable. All isotopes with an atomic number of 83 or greater will eventually break down into smaller pieces. Some transform into completely different elements by the process of **radioactive decay**. The amount of time this transformation takes varies among elements, but it's also a spontaneous or random process.

Think of a microwavable bag of unpopped popcorn kernels. Can you identify exactly which kernels will pop first when the bag heats up? No—it's too random. Yet you can predict about how long it will probably take for most of the kernels in the bag to pop, based on past experience or the manufacturer's guidelines.

Scientists use the term *half-life* (t½) when referring to radioactive decay. This is how long it takes for one-half (50 percent) of the radioactive atoms in an element to break down, from the time measurement begins. Scientists can't predict when an unstable atom will start to decay; they just know it will eventually. By collecting data on a large number of atoms of that element over time, they *can* predict how long the decay process will take once it begins.

The half-life of radium is 1,620 years. So if you had four grams of radium, in 1,620 years you would only have two grams. In another 1,620 years, you would have just one gram, and so on. The number of grams of radium would keep decreasing by half every 1,620 years due to radioactive decay. In comparison, the isotope polonium-210 has a half-life of only 138 days.

However, Marie said, "It is impossible. It would be contrary to the scientific spirit." Pierre agreed. So they quietly decided: if radium could be of use in treating disease, they would not consider taking advantage of their discovery for financial gain! They had chosen poverty and principle over fame and fortune.

But despite their disinterest in becoming celebrities, fame and recognition came to the Curies. They had already gotten a few awards over the years in France. Pierre had received the Gaston Planté Prize in 1895 and the Lacaze Prize in 1901. Marie had received the Gegner Prize three times.

In mid-June 1903, recognition began to come from other countries as well. Pierre was invited to the Royal Institution in England to lecture on radium, and Marie became the first woman ever admitted to a session at the institution. She was not allowed to speak in front of the all-male assembly, but she did get to sit beside her friend Lord Kelvin as she listened to Pierre describe the properties of radium.

Pierre demonstrated how radium affected paper-covered photographic plates, how it gave off heat, and how it glowed in the semi-darkness. Suddenly his scarred hands shook ever so slightly as he tried to hold the test tube steady, and a bit of radium spilled out. Fifty years later, radioactivity from that small

Tasty Decay: Explore the Scientific Concept of a Half-Life

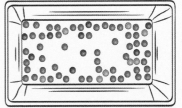

HERE IS A FUN (AND TASTY) way to explore the concept of a half-life and spontaneous/random decay, using candy to represent atoms in radioactive isotopes.

You'll Need
❋ 100 Skittles (or M&Ms)
❋ Rectangular plastic container (shoe box size) with lid
❋ Notebook or graph paper

1. Place each Skittle in the plastic container with the *S* on each candy facing down.

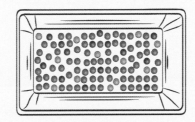

2. Put the lid on the container, hold the container securely, and shake it for a few seconds.

3. Open the container and remove all the candies that now have the *S* facing up. These candies represent atoms that have decayed.

4. Count the remaining Skittles in the container, those that have not "changed."

5. On your paper, record the number of Skittles left unchanged after each attempt. How many attempts did it take for at least half (50) of the candies to change?

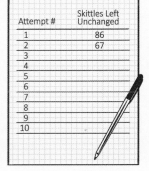

Attempt #	Skittles Left Unchanged
1	86
2	67
3	
4	
5	
6	
7	
8	
9	
10	

6. Continue the procedure until all the candies have turned over and been removed. In this experiment, each shake of the container represents the passage of time using the half-life model.

The turned candies have now all changed into more stable isotopes. Be sure to enjoy a few of these tasty "decayed" treats!

Optional
Create a red line graph using the data you recorded from your experiment.

spill was discovered in the room, and some of the surfaces had to be decontaminated!

Recognition for all Marie's hard work finally came from the Sorbonne as well. Five long years had passed since she began research for her doctoral thesis. She had identified two new elements and successfully isolated pure radium. She had compiled all her original research and findings into a dissertation. Now it was time for her to defend it.

On June 25, 1903, Marie Curie stood before a panel of judges in a little hall of the Sorbonne. Bronya had made the trip to Paris for the presentation, and Marie had even bought herself a new dress for the occasion at her sister's insistence. Pierre, his father, close friends, and several of Marie's Sèvres students were there to show support as well. Marie's biographer later described, "Marie Curie was standing very straight. On her pale face and rounded brow, completely bared by her fair hair brushed back in the crest, a few lines marked the traces of the battle she had fought and won."

The three examiners took turns asking questions about her thesis. Marie answered every question successfully, sometimes drawing a design on the blackboard with chalk, sometimes explaining verbally.

Satisfied with the candidate's performance, Marie's instructor, physicist Gabriel Lippmann, pronounced, "The University of Paris accords you the title of doctor of physical science, with the mention of 'très honorable.'" It was a big day for Marie—she had succeeded!

Several months later, Pierre and Marie learned that the Royal Society of London had awarded them the Davy Medal. Marie was sick and could not attend the ceremony, but Pierre went and brought back the heavy gold medal on which both their names were engraved. And to show just how little he and Marie were concerned with fame or prestige, he gave the medal to Irène to play with.

"Irène adores her big new penny!" he would say to friends who came by.

The Nobel Prize

ON DECEMBER 10, 1903, the Royal Swedish Academy of Sciences announced the current year's Nobel Prize winners. The award in Physics was given jointly to Marie and Pierre Curie and Henri Becquerel for their work with radium. It was another first for Marie! She was the first woman (and the first Polish person) ever to receive a Nobel Prize.

When Pierre had first heard rumblings about nominations earlier in the summer, there had been no mention of Marie's name. However, Pierre made sure the committee knew that Marie deserved full credit for all her hard work and that the nomination should include her as well.

The Curies were not at the ceremony, due to illness, so a French representative received the diplomas and gold medals on their behalf. One of the requirements for winning a Nobel Prize was that the recipients had to make a public lecture in Stockholm within six months following the meeting. The lecture had to be on the subject for which the award was given, and most winners gave their presentations during the days immediately following the award ceremony. Due to their poor health, the Curies' lecture would have to wait.

Pierre wrote to Professor Aurivillius, secretary of the Royal Swedish Academy of Sciences, "We are very grateful to the Academy of Science of Stockholm for the great honor it does us in awarding us half of the Nobel Prize for Physics. We beg you to be kind enough to transmit the expression of our gratitude and of our sincerest thanks."

Alfred Nobel and Nobel Prizes 𝔻

The year Marie Curie was born, 1867, found a Swedish chemist named Alfred Nobel busy securing a patent for a very important explosive—dynamite.

Nobel was born in 1833 in Sweden, but in 1842 his family moved to Russia, where his father was already working as a manufacturer of explosive mines and production tools. He showed a great aptitude for science and chemistry, and he worked with his father until 1859 before returning to Sweden. He built a factory to make a dangerous explosive called nitroglycerin, which can explode if it's slightly jolted. Unfortunately, the factory blew up, killing several people, including his brother. The Swedish government would not let him rebuild the factory, so he continued his work on a barge.

Nobel discovered that the highly sensitive and dangerous liquid nitroglycerin could be handled more safely when mixed with a powdery rock called diatomite. He called his new mixture dynamite. He went on to make more powerful explosives, which made him very wealthy.

Later, Nobel felt guilty that the nitroglycerin he had manufactured had been used in war, as he highly valued peace. He decided to leave his vast fortune as a fund to create annual awards to recognize outstanding work in many scientific and literary fields. Most of all, he wanted to promote peace. These coveted awards were called Nobel Prizes. Alfred Nobel died in 1896.

Portrait of Alfred Bernhard Nobel, originally published in *Harmsworth Popular Science* in 1912.

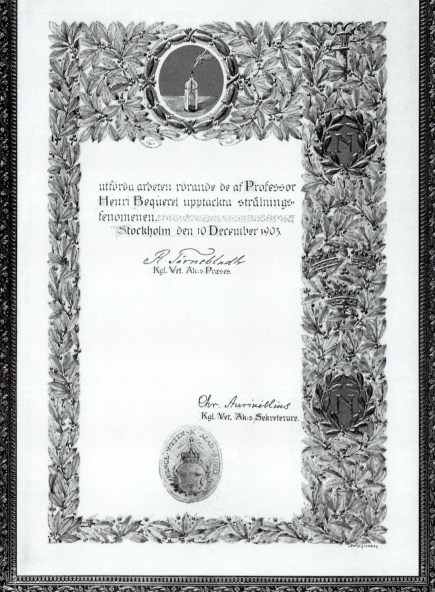

Pierre and Marie shared the 1903 Nobel Prize in Physics with Henri Becquerel. Musée Curie (coll. ACJC)

Their achievement and large cash prize meant that Pierre could be released from his teaching job at the School of Physics and hopefully regain his health. Marie was relieved. Of course, this meant that they would have to leave their Shed of Discovery since Pierre was no longer an employee. One of his former pupils, a well-known physicist named Paul Langevin, replaced him.

The Sorbonne promised to build them the laboratory they had needed and wanted for so long and to create a chair position or physics professor position for Pierre. Pierre was also nominated for membership at the prestigious Academy of Sciences, something he had been denied before. This was all probably bittersweet for the Curies. It had taken a Nobel Prize to get him the chair in physics and the recognition that he deserved in his own country!

The Sorbonne named Marie as Pierre's laboratory chief. She would be the first woman to hold such a position there, so that was a small consolation. And for the first time in her life, she would finally be paid on a regular basis to do scientific research.

In addition to Marie's steady income, the 70,000 gold francs that they received shortly after winning the prize ensured their newfound freedom. Despite their previously poor financial state, however, the Curies were quite generous with this prize money. They loaned

Profile a Nobel Prize Winner

THE PRESTIGIOUS NOBEL PRIZE has been awarded to worthy recipients in the areas of Physics, Chemistry, Medicine, Literature, Peace, and Economic Sciences since 1901. Since that time, the Nobel Prize in Physics has been awarded 108 times to 199 recipients. Wilhelm Röntgen won in 1901 for his discovery of X-rays, and Marie and Pierre Curie shared the 1903 Nobel Prize in Physics with Henri Becquerel for their work with radiation and radioactivity. (Marie won the 1911 Nobel Prize in Chemistry as well.)

A Nobel Prize winner, or laureate, is honored for high achievement in his or her field. A sampling of several well-known Nobel laureates in Physics in the early 1900s includes J. J. Thompson, 1906; Max Planck, 1918; Albert Einstein, 1921; Niels Bohr, 1922; and Enrico Fermi, 1938. Choose one or more recipients of the Nobel Prize in Physics to research, and write up a profile to share at school or with your family.

You'll Need
* Library or Internet access
* Paper and pen or pencil, or computer with word processing software

You can select one of the names provided here, or you can visit www.nobelprize.org to learn about other winners.

Use your local library or the Internet to research the prize winner you've selected.

Use the profile sheet template below or create your own profile layout to record your findings.

NOBEL LAUREATE IN PHYSICS	Photo:
Name:	
Award year:	Interesting facts:
Country:	
Recognized for:	
Year born:	
Year died:	

20,000 Austrian crowns to Bronya and her husband to assist them in establishing their sanatorium, and helped many others in need "without fuss."

Marie's one indulgence was adding a modern bathroom to her home. Other than that, the Curies simply wished to go on as they had before—working uninterrupted in their lab. To the couple, fame was an inconvenience to their work and an interruption to their quiet lifestyle. But life post-radium would never be the same. They received hundreds of letters and requests for interviews.

Marie wrote a letter to her brother, Jozio, telling him about all the photographers and journalists who would not leave them alone. She simply wanted to "dig into the ground somewhere to find a little peace," and she was tired of all the "hubbub."

Moreover, reporters loved to recount the fairy tale story of how the poor little Polish girl turned scientific wonder had married the

Periodic Table of Elements Scavenger Hunt

DID YOU KNOW THAT many of the elements on the periodic table can be found right in your home? Think about it. What do bananas contain? Potassium. Its symbol: K. Its atomic number: 19. Where you can you find iron? In your breakfast cereal. Its symbol: Fe. Its atomic number: 26

You'll Need
❋ A copy of the periodic table of elements (easy to find online or in a science textbook)
❋ Paper
❋ Pen or pencil
❋ Basket or box
❋ Items for elements

Study the periodic table of elements. Then get ready to scavenge.

Read labels on food boxes or cleaning products. Look around your home at building materials or household goods. Collect as many elemental items as you can and place them in your box or basket. For example, a pencil contains graphite—which is a form of carbon. A can of evaporated milk contains calcium. Get creative. It may be easier than you think!

On your printed periodic table, check off each element as you collect a matching item. How many elemental examples did you find? If you want, gather some friends or family members and compete against each other, giving yourselves a time limit. Who can find the most elements in 15 minutes?

brilliant French physicist. It was all too much. Marie was glad that their discoveries would be of benefit to others, but she just wanted her family to be left in peace. However, the world was now fascinated by the Curies and their story.

Her opinion? "In science, we must be interested in things, not in persons."

Pierre's correspondence was an indication of his own irritation. In a letter to a colleague, he said, "People ask me for articles and lectures, and after a few years are passed, the very persons who make these demands will be astonished to see that we have not accomplished any work."

In the summer of 1904, the Curies finally felt well enough to make the trip to Stockholm for the long-delayed Nobel Prize lecture. Although Pierre actually gave the lecture while Marie sat in the audience, he made sure to give her credit for the work she did alone as well as for the work they did together.

By the fall of 1904, Marie and Pierre still did not have the new lab the Sorbonne had promised them. How frustrating! Instead, they had to make do with a two-room laboratory on Rue Cuvier, not far from their previous shed. Still they soldiered on.

Both Curies' health continued to decline. Pierre, especially, seemed affected. Moreover, Marie was expecting another child. In retrospect, given what we know today about the dangers of radium exposure, it's a wonder that Marie had an uncomplicated pregnancy and safe delivery. But she did, and with the birth of their second daughter, Ève Denise, on December 6, 1904, the Curies' life shifted again.

FACING LIFE'S CHALLENGES

The Easter holidays of 1906 were beautiful. Pierre, Marie, and the children took a short vacation in the Chevreuse Valley, and Marie welcomed the days spent away from Paris, enjoying her family. She and Pierre talked about their daughters and their futures. They walked in the meadow and picked flowers. They were peaceful.

> My Pierre, I think of you without end, my head is bursting with it and my reason is troubled. I do not understand that I am to live henceforth without seeing you, without smiling at the sweet companion of my life.
>
> —MARIE CURIE, DIARY ENTRY, MAY 7, 1906

A Tragic Accident

The wagon that killed Pierre had crossed the Pont Neuf (New Bridge) over the Seine River and was entering the narrow, busy Rue Dauphine just as Curie began to cross the street. Author's collection

PIERRE RETURNED home to Paris before his family to attend a reunion and dinner with some of his colleagues on April 17. Marie and the children followed the next day. On April 19, Pierre was scheduled to attend a luncheon for the Sorbonne's Association of Professors in the Faculty of Science and then meet with his publisher, Gauthier-Villars, to correct some manuscript proofs.

The day promised to be rainy. Before he left that morning, Pierre called up the stairs to Marie to ask if she would be going to the laboratory. She replied she was busy and probably would not have time that day. The front door closed, and Pierre hurried away.

After his luncheon, Pierre headed toward his publisher's office. He planned to go work in the laboratory afterward. When he reached his publisher's building, however, he found it closed due to a strike. So he left and began following Rue Dauphine toward the Institut de France, where he planned to do some work in the library.

The noisy street was bustling with horse-drawn wagons, carriages, and trams. It was raining, and pedestrians carrying umbrellas crowded the wet, narrow walkway. Pierre looked for a free path on the asphalt and began to walk behind a covered carriage.

After several minutes, he decided to cross the road. Because of his obstructed view, he did not see the approaching wagon drawn by two horses and carrying a heavy, six-ton load of military uniforms. Lost in his own thoughts, he ran straight into one of the horses. He tried to hang on to it, but the startled animal reared, causing Pierre to slip on the wet pavement and fall right in front of the moving wagon.

The driver tried to stop, but the frightened horses kept going. Miraculously, their feet and the front wheels of the wagon missed Pierre as he lay very still underneath. He was alive! But as the left back wheel of the wagon came over, it crushed his skull. Pierre Curie, the great scientist, lay dead in the muddy Paris street. He was only 46 years old.

The Faculty of Science was notified, and two of the Curies' friends, dean of the faculty Paul Appell and Professor Jean Perrin, hurried to the Curies' house on Boulevard Kellermann to tell Marie the tragic news. Only old Dr. Curie was home when the two men arrived. Because they wanted to notify Marie first, Paul and Jean did not say anything to Eugène about his son's death. He knew by their faces, however, that something was terribly wrong, and guessed.

"My son is dead."

He listened to the account of the accident, and through his grief and tears, he added, "What was he dreaming of this time?"

Marie arrived home at six o'clock. Paul Appell repeated the facts as kindly as he could. The new widow remained so motionless and quiet that the men wondered if she even understood. She did not moan or cry.

"Pierre is dead? Dead? Absolutely dead?" she repeated.

Marie begged for Pierre's body to be brought home. She arranged for Irène to stay with a neighbor. Ève stayed with Marie; she was too young to understand. Then Marie

ÉCRASÉ PAR UN CAMION

MORT TRAGIQUE DE M. CURIE

Le grand savant qui collabora à la découverte du radium a trouvé la mort, hier, sous les roues d'un camion — La science française en deuil.

Le camion meurtrier
(La croix indique la roue qui écrasa le crâne de M. Curie.)

M. ET Mme CURIE
Dans leur laboratoire

Le Matin reported Pierre Curie's accident and death the next day.

sat quietly alone in the back garden as she waited for her assistant, André Debierne, to retrieve Pierre's body from the police station and bring him to her. When her husband was finally stretched out on the floor in front of her, Marie saw that his gentle face was unmarked and peaceful. The rest of his head was bandaged to conceal the gruesome damage.

Marie remained alone with Pierre, kissing his face and holding his hand, until others forced her from the room so they could prepare and dress his body without her having to watch. When she realized what was happen-ing, she raced back into the room and clung to her dead husband.

Ève later wrote that with her father's death, her mother "became not only a widow, but at the same time a pitiful and incurably lonely woman."

Marie arranged for Pierre to be buried in Sceaux in the family tomb, with his mother. To discourage publicity, she moved the date of the burial up to April 21 to avoid a formal procession. However, journalists found out about the plan and hid among nearby tombs to watch. Marie could find no privacy, not even for her grieving.

In the days following the funeral, Eugène Curie, Marie's brother-in-law Jacques, and her siblings Jozio and Bronya stayed with Marie, but they became very concerned. Marie behaved like a robot, moving stiffly from task to task, apparently feeling nothing. She seemed incapable of making decisions. They worried over her future and that of her children. What was to become of them? Ève later wrote, "Stiff, absent-minded, the wife who had not joined the dead seemed already to have abandoned the living."

However, when French government officials offered Marie and her children a national pension, a bit of her fiery spirit kicked in. She refused, saying, "I don't want a pension. I am young enough to earn my living and that of my children." She was only 38.

News of April 1906))

Pierre's death on April 19, 1906, shocked the world. The story of the famous French scientist and his Polish-born wife had intrigued people everywhere, and they were saddened that such a tragic thing could have happened. The French newspaper Le Matin covered Curie's death in great detail, even including a photo of the horse and cart and a map of where the accident took place in the write-up.

American newspapers carried the story on April 20 as well, but it was not front-page news as it was in France. Another event, which took place in California on April 18, overshadowed the news of Pierre's death—the catastrophic San Francisco earthquake.

At 5:13 AM on the 18th, two violent tremors shook the California city, causing thousands of buildings to collapse. That was bad enough, but most of the devastation was caused by the fires that erupted when gas mains were destroyed. The quake and fire resulted in an official count of 700 deaths, 28,000 burned buildings, 250,000 homeless citizens, and close to $500 million in property damages.

For a very brief time after Pierre's death, Marie kept a diary. She wrote mostly to him, and her entries on the tear-stained pages are deeply personal and heartbreaking. Perhaps writing was her way of dealing with grief. Or maybe, as her daughter Ève guessed, she wanted to "fix every detail of the drama which had separated them in order to torture herself with it forever afterward."

Such details are evident in one of Marie's diary passages, which read, "Your hair can hardly be seen, because the wound begins there, and above the forehead, on the right, the bone that broke can be seen."

Most telling of her outlook about her future at that sad time was the entry that said, "Everything is over, Pierre is sleeping his last sleep beneath the earth; it is the end of everything, everything, everything."

Slowly Moving Forward

WHILE MARIE had no interest in working, others wondered about the research work Pierre had left behind and about his teaching position at the Sorbonne. Who would replace him and carry on with his work?

Jacques and Pierre's good friend Georges Gouy approached the dean of faculty. In their opinion, only one person was capable of succeeding Pierre and carrying on his research—his widow, Marie. Traditions and limitations for women must be forgotten, they argued.

On May 13, 1906, the council of the Faculty of Science unanimously decided to give Pierre's position to Marie. She would become a professor of physics and chief of research work at the Sorbonne. This was the first time in French history for a woman to hold a full chair professorship. Her family urged her to take the position, both for herself and for Pierre.

Marie's simple reply? "I will try."

In early autumn, she decided she could no longer live in the house she had shared with Pierre. It was just too sad. So she, her daughters, and her father-in-law moved to a home in Sceaux, the town where Pierre had lived when she met him—and where he was buried. The commute from 6 Rue du Chemin de Fer in Sceaux to her laboratory required her to travel a half hour by train, so she was often gone from early in the morning to late at night.

Marie never showed grief or cried in front of others. She did not want pity or consolation. She never talked about Pierre, not even to her children. If she felt herself losing control or becoming emotional, she would quickly send her daughters out of the room so she could be alone. She held in her feelings, often to the point of harm. One of Ève Curie's first memories is that of seeing her mother collapse in a faint on the dining room floor.

It was also about this time that Marie started rubbing her calloused, scarred fingers (caused by radium burns) against each other in a nervous, almost obsessive tic—a noticeable habit that would last the rest of her life.

Despite her grief, Marie met her obligations. Finally the day arrived for her to present her first lecture as Pierre's successor. A newspaper announced the date, time, and subject of the event. And as the lecture hall started filling early with students, family, close friends, reporters, and curious spectators who wanted to see what Marie would say or do, she was not in Paris but in Sceaux, standing in front of Pierre's tomb. Was she ready? Could she truly fill her husband's big shoes?

At the Sorbonne, Marie walked rapidly to the lecture hall, entered, to the sound of applause, and took her place behind the long table of lab equipment. The audience anticipated a speech about Pierre or, at the very least, a proclamation of how excited or thankful she was for her new position.

But Marie stared straight ahead and simply picked up exactly where Pierre had left off in his last lecture: "When one considers the progress that has been made in physics in the past ten years, one is surprised at the advance

Irène pointing to her mother's radium-scarred fingers. Musée Curie (coll. ACJC)

76

that has taken place in our ideas concerning electricity and matter."

She continued in the same toneless voice through the remainder of the class, then exited the lecture hall as quickly as she had entered, to the sound of more applause and to more than a few tears. History was made that day, and Marie had done as Pierre had requested when he said, "Whatever happens, if one of us has to go on, like a body without a soul, one must work just the same." She had carried on their work "just the same."

A Successful Distraction

AFTER PIERRE'S death, Marie decided she wanted a full hand in Irène's schooling. She did not like the French way of education, which required children to sit all day long in desks, with very little activity. She wanted her children to be active and, like their father when he was a boy, free to enjoy and explore nature.

She recruited close friends, such as the Perrins and the Langevins, who had children the same age as Irène, and together they formed an experimental, informal educational co-op of sorts. There were 10 students, mostly the children of other Sorbonne professors. Along with Marie, some of the parents, and sometimes other scientists, took turns teaching lessons (only one a day) in chemistry, physics,

Marie with Ève (left) and Irène in 1908. Musée Curie (coll. ACJC)

mathematics, history, and French literature. The children did many hands-on experiments and had lots of physical activity. They also went on nature explorations and trips to concerts and museums.

The school experiment lasted two years, and everyone agreed it was highly enjoyable and successful. However, most of the parents were so busy with their own work and teaching schedules that it became impossible to keep the classes going. Therefore, the children began attending official programs. Marie chose to put Irène in the Collège Sévigné, a private school where the classroom hours were limited. It was a good decision. Later, Ève would attend the same school.

Marie Rises to New Challenges

ABOUT FOUR months after Pierre died, Marie was challenged from a totally unexpected person. Pierre's close friend Lord Kelvin publicly stated in a *London Times* article that he did not believe radium was an element. He claimed it was a compound of lead and helium. He also implied the Curies had not deserved a Nobel Prize. Moreover, since Lord Kelvin was such a highly respected scientist, his statement carried great weight.

Marie decided against a public reply. Rather, she determined to work harder to prove herself. She and Pierre had isolated **radium chloride**, the purified form of radium salt, but her new plan was to produce pure **metallic radium**. The task seemed almost impossible, but her anger at Lord Kelvin's accusation and feelings of injustice drove her forward.

Fortunately for Marie, the American steel millionaire and philanthropist Andrew Carnegie of Pennsylvania donated $50,000 to the Sorbonne in 1907, money which was to be earmarked specifically for her work. The donation provided funding for Marie's laboratory as well as a series of annual research fellowships for gifted students. Her nephew, Jacques's son Maurice, was among the recipients.

The process to produce pure metallic radium took her four years, but in 1910, with the help of her faithful assistant, André, Marie was finally able to isolate a few grains of pure radium metal (worth around $3 million an ounce) using a complicated procedure, which she never repeated, due to the danger of losing too much radium in the process. Therefore, despite all the effort to obtain the pure radium, she "could not keep it in this state, for it was required for further experiments."

Working on her own, Marie was also able to devise a more accurate method of measuring radium by measuring the radioactive rays it gave off or emanated. The existence of the element was indisputable. Unfortunately, Lord

Kelvin died before he found out his accusation was way off the mark.

In addition to solving a scientific challenge, Marie had to face a new personal challenge in 1910. Her father-in-law, Dr. Eugène Curie, had been a comfort and help to her in the years following Pierre's death. She was gone long hours, so old Dr. Curie became her daughters' chief caretaker, playmate, and confidante in their mother's absence. In fact, he was Irène's very best friend. This gentle, blue-eyed grandfather influenced her intellectual and spiritual mind and political views more than anyone else.

In 1909, Dr. Curie had developed a lung condition that kept him in bed for a year. Then on February 25, 1910, the beloved man passed away. Marie had his coffin placed beneath Pierre's in the family tomb. She was heartbroken, and Irène was devastated. The Polish governesses who took over the girls' care would never take their grandfather's place in their hearts.

Lord Kelvin (1824–1907) 🔊

William Thompson, known as First Baron Kelvin or Lord Kelvin, was an Irish physicist and mathematician who is remembered for his outstanding achievements in the fields of physics and mechanics. Widely recognized and highly respected both in the world of science and in society, Lord Kelvin was the first to discover the concept of absolute zero in temperature, and the Kelvin scale is named after him.

He formulated the first and second laws of thermodynamics and worked extensively with mathematics and electricity. Kelvin was the first scientist ever to join the House of Lords in England. He also took an interest in engineering and was actively involved in laying the first transatlantic cable. He is known for improving adjustable compasses and helping design the power station at Niagara Falls in New York.

Lord Kelvin is remembered as one of the greatest scientists of all time. His contributions as a physicist, mathematician, engineer, and inventor are almost unparalleled. Some say he was the Isaac Newton of his era, so it was most fitting that he was buried beside Newton at Westminster Abbey in 1907.

William Thompson, Lord Kelvin.

The Kelvin Scale and Temperature Conversion

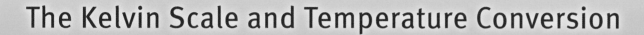

ALTHOUGH THE GENERAL PUBLIC most often use the Fahrenheit and Celsius temperature scales, scientists widely use the Kelvin scale, which is the standard metric system of temperature measurement.

Both the Celsius and Kelvin scales use 100 equal degree increments between the freezing and boiling points. However, the absolute-zero mark (the lowest temperature that can be achieved) on the Kelvin scale is 273.15 units cooler than the Celsius. Additionally, the Kelvin scale doesn't measure in degrees, as the Fahrenheit and Celsius scales do. That is, 400 units above absolute zero on a Kelvin scale is written as 400 Kelvin instead of 400 degrees Kelvin.

You can use simple conversion equations to make comparisons between the three scales:

$$°C = K - 273.15$$
$$°F = °C \times + 32$$
$$K = °C + 273.15$$

You'll Need
※ Paper and pen or pencil, or calculator

Using the equations at left, see if you can make the conversions for the most common temperature measurements, including:
※ Absolute zero
※ The freezing point of water
※ Room temperature
※ The average human body temperature
※ The boiling point of water

For example: To find the boiling point of water on the Celsius scale, take the given temperature on the Kelvin scale and plug it into the formula $°C = K - 273.15$ for the answer.

$$°C = 373.15K - 273.15 \text{ or}$$

$$
\begin{array}{r}
373.15 \text{ K} \\
- 273.15 \\
\hline
100.00°C
\end{array}
$$

Kelvin (K)	Celsius (°C)	Fahrenheit (°F)	
373.15K	?	?	*Boiling point of water*
?	37°	?	*Average body temperature*
?	?	77°	*Room temperature*
?	?	32°	*Freezing point of water*
0K	?	?	*Absolute zero*

Like her own mother, Marie did not show a lot of affection to her daughters, but she loved them deeply. In her mind, she was protecting them from suffering. If they, too, were insensitive and undemonstrative, she reasoned, perhaps they would be less likely to experience the same levels of pain and heartache she herself had suffered through the years. Yet as she tried to make her children invulnerable, her daughter Ève felt Marie was "too tender, too delicate, too much gifted for suffering" and "shriveled with grief at the least sign of indifference."

Marie did encourage her daughters' strengths and talents. Irène showed early on that she, like her parents, had an aptitude for science, as she would most certainly prove later on. Ève was talented in music and writing.

Facing Scandal

MARIE HAD written and published many documents about her work and research, including the two-volume set titled *Treatise on Radioactivity*. She was a well-recognized scientist. She kept up with all the latest scientific research and discoveries, and she was friend and colleague to such men as Albert Einstein and Ernest Rutherford. She was respected in her field.

So when friends urged her to offer herself as a candidate into the prestigious French Academy of Sciences, she agreed. Since a woman had never been elected, public interest was aroused. Would members of this influential scientific organization actually vote her in? When the election votes were counted, Marie had lost by just one. She never again submitted her name for membership, nor did she ever present any of her work to the academy in the future.

Marie may have been frustrated at not being admitted into the Academy of Sciences, as Pierre had been. But this disappointment was surely overshadowed by a brewing scandal.

In October 1911, Paris newspapers were filled with rumors about Marie and her fellow physicist, mathematician, and friend Paul Langevin. She was accused of having a romantic relationship with Langevin, who had been separated from his wife and living apart from his family for some time. Langevin's wife claimed that Marie had broken up their marriage—and said she had proof in the letters Marie and Paul had written to one another.

Marie's friends and family rushed to her defense, but it seemed that most of Paris turned against her. Daily headlines about the scandal continued, and people called her names and even threatened to attack her. For a time, Marie was afraid for her life and the safety of her children, so she and the girls stayed with friends to avoid confrontation and publicity.

Paul Langevin at Cambridge University, England, in 1897.
André Langevin family archives, Wikimedia Commons

Make an Atomic Model of Carbon

ATOMIC THEORY HAS CHANGED through the years, from John Dalton's belief that all matter was made up of small atoms and each element had its own type of atom to today's quantum physics electron cloud model.

Check out the atomic model time line below.

In this activity, you will make an atomic model for the element carbon (C). The atomic number for carbon is 6, which indicates its number of protons. Carbon's atomic mass is 12, which is the mass of protons plus the mass of neutrons in the nucleus. Carbon will also have six electrons, because the number of electrons always equals the number of protons in an elemental atom to balance the charge.

You'll Need

※ 12 Styrofoam 2-inch (5-cm) balls

※ 6 Styrofoam 1-inch (2½-cm) balls

※ 3 colors of acrylic paint

※ Paintbrush

※ Black permanent marker

※ Toothpicks or glue

※ 6 wooden skewers, cut to varying lengths (between 6 and 8 inches [15–20 cm])

1. Paint six of the larger balls one color, and the other six large balls another color. Paint the six smaller balls a third color. The two sets of large balls represent protons (+) and neutrons (no charge). The smaller balls represent electrons (–). Set them aside to dry.

2. After the painted balls are dry, use a permanent marker to draw a + on the protons and a – on the electrons. The neutrons won't be marked.

3. Use short sections of toothpicks or glue to attach your protons and neutrons together to form carbon's nucleus.

4. Stick one end of each skewer segment into an electron. Stick the other end of each skewer into either a proton or neutron in the nucleus clump, arranging the electrons to create a cloud surrounding the atom's nucleus.

Extra Challenge

Research the element carbon. Describe its history and uses.

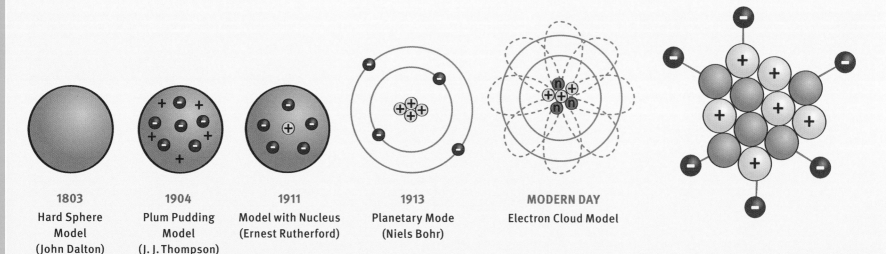

1803	1904	1911	1913	MODERN DAY
Hard Sphere Model (John Dalton)	Plum Pudding Model (J. J. Thompson)	Model with Nucleus (Ernest Rutherford)	Planetary Mode (Niels Bohr)	Electron Cloud Model

Finally she had enough. She did not admit to having a relationship with Langevin, and in fact, she wrote a public response in a publication called *Le Temps*, threatening to take legal action against the press, if needed.

But the damage to her reputation had been done. Despite all of her successes and fame, many called for her dismissal from the Sorbonne. Since many of her close friends were in influential positions at the university, Marie was able to keep her job. However, in the middle of the chaos, the University of Warsaw offered her a position in Poland, and her family urged her to take it. But despite how much she had once longed to return to her home country, Marie would not be run out of France! She was determined to stay in Paris and work, even though she had been humiliated by the press and most of the citizens disliked her.

The effects of the scandal lingered. In November 1911, Marie received two telegrams from Sweden. The first one informed her that she had been awarded another Nobel Prize, this time in Chemistry, for discovering the elements of radium and polonium and for isolating pure radium in its metallic form. The second telegram was from a member on the Nobel committee advising her not to come to Stockholm to receive her award, due to the Langevin scandal.

Marie was insulted and quickly fired back a letter of reply informing the writer that there was no connection between her private life and her work. She would be accepting her award in person!

Taking Bronya and Irène with her for support, Marie traveled to Sweden to pick up her prize and deliver her lecture—becoming the first woman in history to give a Nobel Prize speech. She was careful to acknowledge others, including Pierre, for their part in the work, but she also gave herself full credit for the accomplishments and research she had done on her own.

The Radium Institute

MARIE BECAME the only person ever to receive two Nobel Prizes in two different sciences, but the price she paid was steep. She was sick the entire trip and had lost a lot of weight. When she returned to Paris, she was admitted to a private hospital under a false name for severe kidney problems that required surgery.

She was so ill that she thought she was going to die. She even wrote a seven-page letter detailing what she wanted done with the radium in her possession in the case of her death. After the surgery, Marie spent almost a year recovering before returning to her work. She spent part of this time at the home of scientist Hertha Ayrton in England and also visited with Albert Einstein and his family.

Albert Einstein: The Patent Clerk 🎧

Albert Einstein's name is synonymous with the word *genius*, not to mention wild, unruly hair. He is famous for his theory of relativity and its resulting $E = mc^2$ formula explaining that energy equals mass times the velocity of light squared. Yet Einstein began his amazing intellectual career as the lowest-paid clerk in a patent office!

Born on March 14, 1879, in Germany, Albert was the son of Jewish parents, although they were nonpracticing Jews. They highly valued education and knowledge, and Albert displayed an interest in science when he was very young. He completed his primary and secondary schooling in Germany and Switzerland, and at the age of 17, he enrolled in the four-year Zurich Polytechnic teaching program to study physics and mathematics. He received his teaching degree in 1900 and then spent two years unsuccessfully trying to find a teaching job. Luckily, a classmate's father was able to help him get an entry-level job at the Swiss Federal Institute of Intellectual Property patent office.

However, he never ceased to be a thinker and dreamer. He questioned everything. What if...? How about...? Will this...? Albert finished his patent work as quickly as he could each day, then used the rest of the time to pursue his own ideas. Amazingly, he published four of his most groundbreaking papers on the photoelectric effect, Brownian motion, special relativity, and the equivalence of mass and energy while working at the patent office.

Just as Marie Curie did, this Nobel Prize–winning genius proved that humble beginnings did not limit a successful future.

Einstein in Caputh, Germany, 1931.
Library of Congress, Prints and Photographs Division (LC-USZ-4940)

Through their work, Einstein and Curie had become friends. He supported and defended her during the Langevin ordeal and had sent this encouraging (and somewhat humorous) letter on November 23, 1911:

Highly esteemed Mrs. Curie,

Do not laugh at me for writing you without having anything sensible to say. But I am so enraged by the base manner in which the public is presently daring to concern itself with you that I absolutely must give vent to this feeling. However, I am convinced that you consistently despise this rabble.... I am impelled to tell you how much I have come to admire your intellect, your drive, and your honesty, and that I consider myself lucky to have made your personal acquaintance.... If the rabble continues to occupy itself with you, then simply don't read that hogwash, but rather leave it to the reptile for whom it has been fabricated.

With most amicable regards to you, Langevin, and Perrin, yours very truly,

A. Einstein

By the fall of 1912, the scandal surrounding Marie had finally died down, she had recovered from her kidney surgery, and she was ready to move on. She helped establish a standard measurement for radium's radioactivity. And she wanted the "standard" sample of radium to be kept at *her* lab since she was the one who had discovered it.

Additionally, a new project was in the works. The Pasteur Institute had joined the Sorbonne University, and a new laboratory was to be built. It would be called the Radium Institute, and its address would be on a street named in honor of Pierre and Marie. One part of the institute would be a laboratory for Marie to carry on her radium research. The other part would be the Pasteur laboratory, where researchers would study uses of radium in cancer treatment.

Sadly, Marie and Pierre's Shed of Discovery had to be torn down during the new construction, but Marie knew her husband would have been ecstatic over the new laboratory.

By July 1914, the Radium Institute was complete. Marie and her assistants began moving their equipment in and making plans for new research on radioactivity. But big trouble was brewing in Europe, and the advent of World War I would change Marie's plans quite dramatically.

The Radium Institute

In 1909, the Sorbonne and the Pasteur Institute joined forces to create the Radium Institute, and construction of a new facility began in 1912. This Institut du Radium was divided into two parts—the Curie laboratory and the Pasteur laboratory. Marie directed the chemistry and physics research in her quarters, and Dr. Claudius Regaud was the director of the other lab, where biological research and the study of medical effects of radioactivity took place. It was a good partnership.

In 1920, Marie and Claudius started the Curie Foundation to help fund the institute. Thanks to the money raised, the first hospital at the Radium Institute was opened in 1922, and Dr. Regaud and his team were able to begin using new treatments and radium therapy on cancer patients. Both labs continued to grow in size and influence, and the Curie Lab became the hub for French science.

The Curie Foundation and the Radium Institute merged in 1970 to become the Curie Institute (Institut Curie), which has three foundational missions—research, cancer treatment, and teaching. Today the organization is one of the leading cancer research centers in the world.

7

WORLD WAR I AND THE "LITTLE CURIES"

Marie had rented a seaside vacation villa in Brittany, in north-western France, for the summer of 1914. Irène, Ève, their governess, and a cook were already there, and Marie was planning to join them in late July or early August. However, an event in faraway Sarajevo, Bosnia, changed her plans. The heir to the Austro-Hungarian throne and his wife were assassinated, setting into motion the events leading up to World War I, or the Great War, as it was called in Marie's lifetime. Before long, France was under attack by Germany.

The theater of war is changing at the moment; the enemy seems to be going farther away from Paris. We are all hopeful, and we have faith in the final success.

—MARIE CURIE, IN A LETTER TO HER DAUGHTER IRÈNE, SEPTEMBER 6, 1914

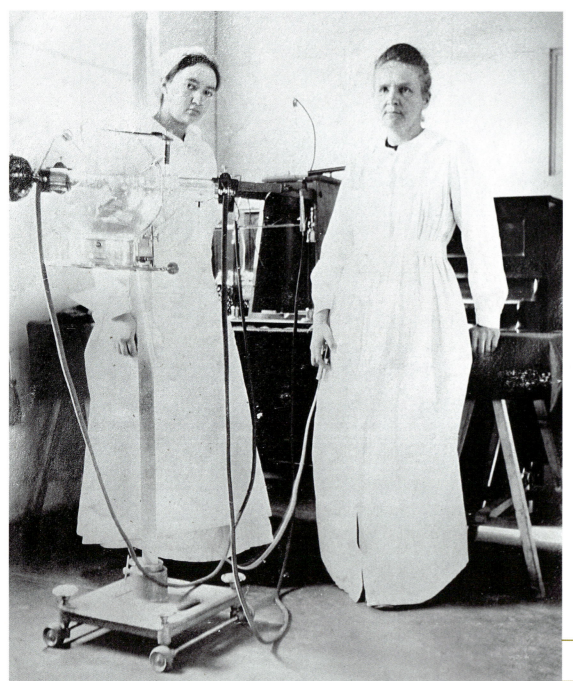

War Effort

AS TROOPS headed toward them, many Parisians feared German occupation. The French government decided to move all of its government offices to a safer location, in Bordeaux, in the South of France.

With the declaration of war on France, almost all of Marie's laboratory staff and many of her students were mobilized. In addition, many residents of Paris fled the city. However, Marie thought that most of the Parisians "gave a strong impression of calm and quiet decision in that fateful year of 1914."

Marie considered her options and then made her own quiet decision as well. Although she would not leave Paris herself, she wanted her daughters to remain in Brittany, where they were safe. Irène, who was almost 17, was not happy with the separation, and she made sure her mother knew it.

On August 6, Marie responded to her daughter, "My dear Irène, I too want to bring you back here, but it is impossible at the moment. Be patient."

Although she was concerned about her daughters and her family in Poland, Marie was not anxious about her own safety. She was, instead, worried about the gram (about

Irène and Marie at a field hospital in 1915.
Musée Curie (coll. ACJC)

half a teaspoon) of radium that she had donated to the Radium Institute and was being kept in her lab. She had been charged with its safekeeping and did not plan to have it fall into enemy hands.

By 1914, radium had become a very precious and extremely expensive commodity due to its medical and commercial value and difficulty to prepare. Therefore, the government wanted its national treasure taken to Bordeaux as a safety measure.

Of course, Marie would not trust the important errand to anyone else, so she decided to transport the radium herself. She packed it in a lead container and boarded a train for the South of France. The 20-gram (45-pound) lead container was so heavy she could not lift it without help. Nevertheless, undeterred, she

Assassination of Archduke Franz Ferdinand 𝕯𝕴

On June 28, 1914, Archduke Francis Ferdinand, heir to the Austro-Hungarian throne, and his wife, Sophie, were shot by a Bosnian Serb revolutionary named Gavrilo Princip while they visited the Bosnian city of Sarajevo. The assassination was planned by a society called Young Bosnia, whose goal was to separate Bosnia from the Austro-Hungarian Empire and join the Kingdom of Serbia. Of course, Austria sought revenge for the assassination!

On July 28, 1914, Austria-Hungary officially declared war on Serbia and invaded the country. Suddenly, entangled and complex decades-old European alliances were brought into play, and before long many countries were involved. Russia and France went to the aid of the Serbs, which caused Germany to rise up to help Austria-Hungary by declaring war on Russia and France. This caused England to declare war on Germany. World War I—or the Great War, as it was then called—had officially begun.

Archduke Franz Ferdinand and his wife, Sophie, were assassinated in Sarajevo on June 28, 1914, and this event triggered World War I. Their three children (left to right), Ernst, Max, and Sophie (named for her mother) became the first orphans of the war.
Library of Congress Prints and Photographs Division, George Grantham Bain Collection (LC-B2- 3000-11)

delivered the radium to a bank vault in Bordeaux and returned to Paris the next day on a train full of soldiers.

After her return, Marie found out that the German advance had been broken and the Battle of the Marne had begun. Paris was saved! So in September, Marie finally sent for her daughters, who were happy to return home after being separated from their mother since early summer. Ève went back to school, and Irène took a course to receive a nursing diploma.

Marie on the Front Lines

ONCE THE radium was safe in Bordeaux and her daughters were home, Marie looked around to see what else she could do to help her adopted country with the war effort. She figured that France needed money and gold to finance the war effort. So she used a large part of her Nobel Prize money to buy French war bonds, even though she knew they would probably be worthless after the war. She also tried to donate her gold medals, but officials at the Bank of France "indignantly refused to send the glorious medals to be melted up." Far from being flattered, Marie thought the officials' decision was ridiculous.

Marie also realized that with the growing severity of fighting and deadly battles, more and more soldiers would have to be operated on near the front—and quickly. X-ray equipment could help surgeons pinpoint where bullets and shrapnel were embedded in the soldiers' flesh, the exact location of a broken bone, or a damaged organ. This ability to see inside human bodies and make informed decisions before operating was certain to save more lives.

At the beginning of the war, however, Marie discovered that the Military Board of

Radiology in the War 𝄞

When World War I began, the need for radiology units at the front became apparent. More lives could be saved if doctors could identify where bullets or shrapnel entered a soldier's body, where the break in a bone was located, or if a vital organ was damaged. Marie's contribution of helping to outfit radiology cars and establish radiological units near the battlefront was invaluable.

There were a few problems though. Radiology technicians could not regulate a consistent energy level of radiation. Moreover, it was hard to keep the plate and patient still during the long exposure time. This resulted in fogging of the glass from scatter radiation. Additionally, the glass photographic plates were easily broken during transport of the radiological equipment. When George Eastman introduced film in 1918, doctors and radiology technicians were some of the first to show interest.

Because no one recognized the dangers of radiation poisoning, many of the people who worked with early X-rays, or **radiographs**, suffered radiation burns or hair loss, or developed cancer. Many years would pass before safety measures to limit radiation exposure would be put into practice.

The men and women who worked with radiological equipment in World War I put their own lives and health in jeopardy to save the lives of others. Although they probably never realized it, they were heroes too!

Health had no organization for mobile radiology. There were several radiology specialists and some equipment in a few important city hospitals, but X-rays were not used on a wide scale—and certainly not at the field hospitals near the battlefronts, where they were most needed. Mobile X-ray units, or radiological cars, were a must.

Marie had found the job for her. As a physicist, she was knowledgeable about X-rays and had even given lectures about them, but she had never taken one herself. So she learned. Then she taught Irène and several others how to use the X-ray machines. From 1916 to 1918, more than 150 individuals were trained as radiological technicians.

First, Marie gathered up all the X-ray equipment she could find in labs or stores. Then, aided by the Red Cross, she had a Renault truck converted into a radiological unit that could carry equipment to the front lines. When she received a telegram or phone call, she would hop into the Renault and a driver would take her to a field hospital. They could set everything up in about a half hour, and then Marie would take X-rays as long as she was needed. It might take hours or days before she returned home, depending on the length of the battle and number of wounded soldiers.

After a while, Marie realized two things: (1) She needed to learn how to drive and do minor auto repairs on the radiological car her-

Marie driving a radiological car in 1914. She also learned to make repairs herself.
Musée Curie (coll. ACJC)

self. Although women drivers were rare at the time, she was determined. (2) There needed to be more radiological rooms and more outfitted radiological units that could be driven to the front lines.

Marie decided to find more cars or trucks that could be converted into mobile X-ray units. Her daughter Ève referred to this task of getting past the government's red tape as Marie's method of "getting on with it." In her gentle yet determined way, Marie approached

Make a "Little Curie"

MARIE'S FIRST RADIOLOGICAL UNIT was a converted Renault truck. With help from the Red Cross, she was able to outfit it for the job of carrying X-ray equipment to the front during World War I. Later, her team borrowed other cars and converted these into "Little Curies" as well.

In this activity, you can make a model of a Little Curie.

Adult supervision required

You'll Need

※ 4-by-6-inch (10-by-15-cm) box, reinforced by tape if necessary
※ Ruler
※ Scissors or box cutter
※ Clear packaging tape
※ 7-by-7-inch (18-by-18-cm) piece of thin cardboard
※ Gray, black, white, and red acrylic paint
※ Paintbrush
※ 2 wooden skewers, 5 inches (13 cm) long
※ White cardstock
※ Glue

1. With adult supervision, use sharp scissors or a box cutter to make incisions along three edges and across the top of the box to cut away a 1½-by-4-inch (4-by-10-cm) section from the box top.

2. Create flaps on the long sides of the box by making a slit starting at each cutaway corner and cutting 1½ inches (4 cm) down (four slits total).

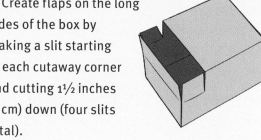

3. Fold down the side flaps, fold in the front flap, and secure everything with tape.

4. Cut four equal-sized (about 2-inch [5- cm] diameter) circles from a thin sheet of cardboard to create tires.

5. Paint the automobile with the gray acrylic paint and set aside to dry. You can also paint white headlights on the front and rectangular black doors on each side.

6. Paint the wheel circles black and set aside to dry.

7. Mark where each wheel should go on the truck sides, using a ruler to ensure equidistance on both sides of the

truck. Using the sharp tip of the scissors or box cutter, punch a hole where you marked.

8. Push a wooden skewer through the front hole on one side, through to the front hole on the other side. Do the same for the back holes. Adjust the length of the skewers if necessary.

9. Push the wheels onto the skewer axels on each side. You may have to punch holes in the cardboard circles first.

10. Cut two white circles from cardstock and paint a Red Cross symbol in the center of each. When dry, glue them on each side of the Little Curie's body.

generous Parisian women to give or lend their limousines, with the slightly mocking assurance "I shall give you back your motor car after the war. Truthfully, if it's not useless by then, I shall give it back to you!"

Marie then transformed the cars into mobile X-ray units, nicknamed "Little Curies" in the army zones. For the most part, she and her workers were a welcome sight on the front lines. But the work of a traveling radiologist

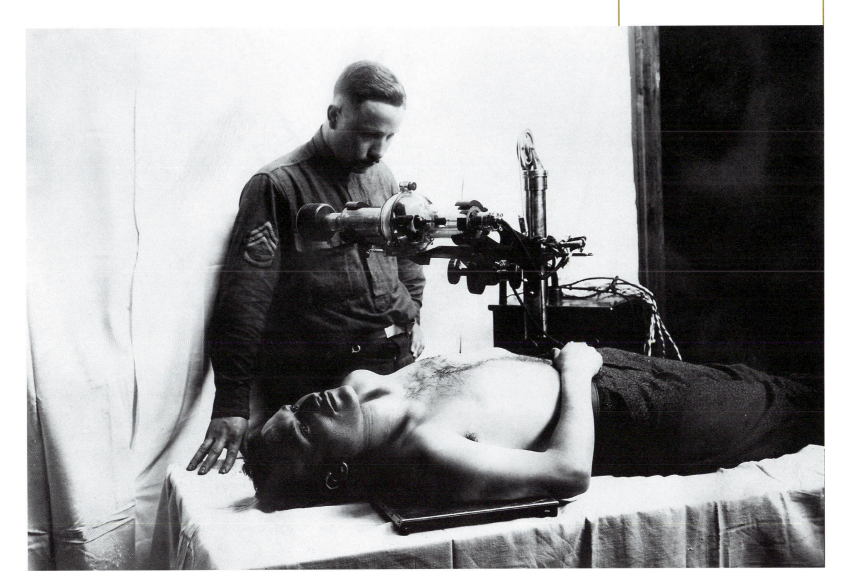

Read Real World War I X-Rays

THE SCIENCE OF RADIOLOGY has come a long way since World War I. Today we have all kinds of technology and medical imaging systems to diagnose and treat injuries and illnesses. But what if you had been a doctor, medic, or X-ray technician in 1917? Would you have been able to look at a radiological image and pinpoint specific problems? Find out in this activity!

Try to read these actual World War I X-rays and form a diagnosis for each. Hints: Try to guess which body parts are shown in the X-rays. Refer to a skeletal system picture if you get stuck. What might the light and dark places indicate? Do you see any unusual looking objects in the images?

Compare your diagnoses to the actual World War I doctors' diagnoses and notes at right.

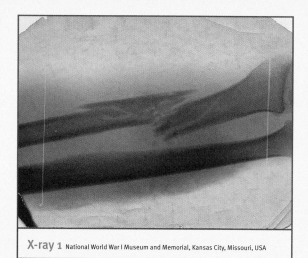

X-ray 1 National World War I Museum and Memorial, Kansas City, Missouri, USA

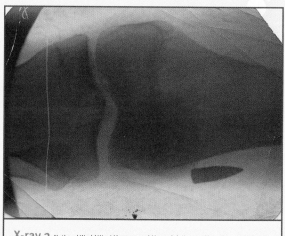

X-ray 2 National World War I Museum and Memorial, Kansas City, Missouri, USA

X-ray 1 diagnosis: Fractured radius and wound of a soldier's left arm, caused by rifle bullet.

Doctor's note: Good condition. Entrance wound, small diameter, radial side of left forearm, about 6 cm above end of radius. Exit on external surface, about 3 × 5 cm in size, draining pus. Fracture of radius.

X-ray 2 diagnosis: Bullet wound and injury to a soldier's right leg and knee; the bullet is still lodged in the flesh. The kneecap is slightly displaced.

Doctor's note: Wounded Feb. 2 in right leg. Good condition. Entrance—outer side of right lower leg; knee swollen. X-ray—slight injury to upper part of right thigh. Undeformed bullet lodged at lower outer condyle (rounded projection of a bone) of femur. Patella displaced, slightly upward.

Treatment: Possible splint, patella drawn down by bandage.

could be grueling and dangerous. In addition to facing enemy fire and explosions, driving on the rough, muddy, bumpy roads was a hazard. On one occasion, Marie was actually thrown out of a radiological car when her driver accidentally overturned it in a ditch.

However, many men and women performed their duties with courage and skill. Irène became so capable that she began working independently from her mother and even trained other radiologists. This was very beneficial to Marie, who was determined to have a well-run organization.

By 1916, Marie had been named director of the Red Cross Radiological Service. And by all accounts, she was able to equip 20 motor cars as radiological units and install 200 radiological rooms, actions that helped over a million wounded men during the war.

Radium's Uses in the War

MARIE HAD been able to retrieve the radium from Bordeaux in 1915, bring it back to her lab at the Radium Institute, and put it to work helping the wounded and sick during World War I. She did not intend to risk the loss of the actual limited quantity of radium itself but rather one of its emanations, which was a stable by-product. In the years since she and Pierre had discovered the element, it was determined that **radon**, the gas given off by

The Women of World War I 🔊

As men went off to fight during World War I, women were recruited to work the jobs the men left behind in factories, medical offices, shipyards, businesses, stores, public works, banks, and so on. Women were also needed to fill positions as stenographers, telegraphers, reporters, journalists, and phone operators, as well as to assume duties such as those of ticket conductors, chauffeurs, mechanics, elevator operators, and more.

Work in powder and ammunition factories was especially important, as were the jobs on farms. Ammunition and food were key components to winning the war! The British Women's Land Army was one program that recruited women to work on farms and help produce crops. Other women opened their homes as hospitals and convalescent centers for wounded soldiers returning from the war.

Women also continued to work as nurses or nurses' aides on the home front, as well as near the battlefront. A smaller number of women even served their countries *on* the battlefront, most disguised as men but with some Eastern European women fighting openly, such as the Russian "Women's Battalion of Death." Like Marie, some women worked as radiology or medical technicians, while others drove ambulances to move the wounded men from place to place. Volunteers with organizations such as the Red Cross, YWCA, and Patriotic League were familiar faces, and their tireless dedication to serving the men and women near the front lines provided encouragement and assistance in an otherwise bleak environment.

radium, could be used to treat scar tissue and skin cancer.

Using radon was much more practical than using the radium itself, as it had a half-life of less than four days and could be collected at regular intervals. Marie used a method developed by an Irish scientist, John Joly, to draw off the gas from the radium and collect it in tiny glass tubes. The tubes could then be

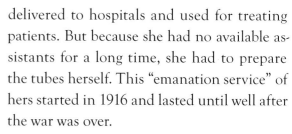

Write a World War I Medic Journal Entry or Letter

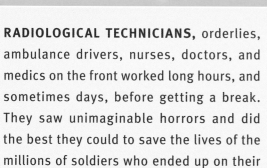

RADIOLOGICAL TECHNICIANS, orderlies, ambulance drivers, nurses, doctors, and medics on the front worked long hours, and sometimes days, before getting a break. They saw unimaginable horrors and did the best they could to save the lives of the millions of soldiers who ended up on their stretchers, in their ambulances, on cots in their tents or wards, or on their operating tables.

In this activity, you are to take on the role of a doctor, medic, nurse, orderly, or aide in a clearing station at the battlefront and write about your experiences.

You'll Need
* Library or Internet access
* Paper and pen or pencil, or computer with word processing software

Do online research and read diaries, journals, or books about medical practices at the front during World War I.

Some good online sources to learn more about World War I are:

* Imperial War Museums—World War I: www.iwm.org.uk/history/first-world -war
* The National World War I Museum and Memorial: www.theworldwar.org
* The Library of Congress Guide to World War I Materials: www.loc.gov/rr /program/bib/wwi/wwi.html

Some recommended books are:

* *Medicine on the Battlefield* by M. M. Eboch (Essential Library)
* *Women Heroes of World War I* by Kathryn J. Atwood (Chicago Review Press)
* *World War I for Kids* by R. Kent Rasmussen (Chicago Review Press)

After your research, imagine you are working in the war. Think about what other medical professionals you read about did during the war. What were their duties? What did they see and feel? Write a journal entry or letter describing your work and the devastation around you.

delivered to hospitals and used for treating patients. But because she had no available assistants for a long time, she had to prepare the tubes herself. This "emanation service" of hers started in 1916 and lasted until well after the war was over.

Radium also helped in more practical ways during wartime, although no one realized its dangers at the time. Radium-based paint, which could glow in the dark, was used to paint numerals on the clock faces of wristwatches. This allowed soldiers to see the time even in the darkest trenches. The paint was also used to highlight the dials on instruments in ships, planes, and tanks.

Peace at Last

ALTHOUGH MARIE continued to show a cheerful face to her comrades throughout the war, her inner thoughts were much different. She worried about the loss of time from her research and work, and about her family in Poland, from whom she'd had no word. She also carried the horrible memories of the wounded, suffering, dying, and dead soldiers she had seen for the rest of her life.

When the war finally ended in November 1918 with a victory for the Allies (the group that consisted of countries including England, France, Italy, and the United States), Marie was relieved and happy. And for the little Polish girl who still lived inside of the grown-up physicist, there were two victories to celebrate. After years of oppression, Poland was once again a free (and recognized) country! Marie's lifelong "patriotic dream" was a reality.

As she wrote to her brother, Jozio, in December 1920, "So now we, 'born in servitude and chained since birth,' we have seen that resurrection of our country which has been our dream. We did not hope to live to see this moment ourselves; we thought it might not even be given to our children to see it—and it is here!"

At the end of the letter were these words: "Like you, I have faith in the future."

The four years of war had put their stamp on Marie's life. She was tired. She had lost her money through purchasing war bonds. She was beginning to admit that exposure to radium and radiation might be causing her health problems. And she still mourned Pierre and the life they had shared.

But through her tireless efforts and knowledge, she had helped to change and improve French battlefield medicine forever. And now that the Great War was over, it was time to get back to work in her lab.

MARIE'S LATER YEARS

8

Now that the war was over and Poland was free, Marie was ready to return to the lab—and ready to get back into the scientific research game. Unfortunately, much of her lab equipment was gone and many of her students and research assistants had yet to return. Nevertheless, she taught her classes and even wrote a book called *Radiology in War*, about her wartime experiences with X-ray technology.

Up until this point, Marie had refused to waste time with public relations, but now she reconsidered. She would give interviews in order to make money, but only under one condition—no personal questions allowed.

> I got back to France with a feeling of gratitude for the precious gift of the American women, and with a feeling of affection for their great country tied with ours by a mutual sympathy which gives confidence in a peaceful future for humanity.
>
> —Marie Curie, on her trip to America

Marie Meets America

IN MAY 1920, an editor and journalist from New York named Missy Meloney interviewed Marie in her laboratory. As they talked about Marie's work, Missy asked questions about royalties on patents, which surely must have made Marie very wealthy. Quietly Marie responded, "Radium was not to enrich anyone. Radium is an element. It belongs to all the people."

Missy also discovered that there was only one gram of radium in France. It was the gram that Marie and Pierre had produced, and it was the property of the Radium Institute and strictly for hospital use in cancer treatment, not research.

The American journalist was shocked. The woman who had discovered radium and worked tirelessly to isolate and produce it had none to use for her own research! Moreover, since one gram of radium cost $100,000, Marie certainly could not afford to buy any.

Missy knew that many Americans, especially women, were some of Marie's biggest fans and would probably want to help. They considered Marie to be a role model and pioneer for women's rights. Missy soon came up

Marie standing in her lab at the Radium Institute. Musée Curie (coll. ACJC)

with the idea for a campaign to raise enough money to buy a gram of radium for Marie.

Once back in America, Missy wrote an article about Marie in the *Delineator* and asked for donations to help buy a gram of radium for the renowned Marie Curie. The campaign was a success and netted around $150,000 in less than a year. Standard Chemical Company produced the radium, and 54-year-old Marie agreed to Missy's request that she and her daughters come to America in May 1921 to personally accept the generous gift from President Warren G. Harding at a White House reception.

Of course, Irène and Ève were excited about the adventure, but Marie had to overcome her fears and natural reserve in order to begin the six-week journey. With Missy as their escort, the Curie women set sail to America aboard the SS *Olympic*, sister ship to the ill-fated SS *Titanic*. They arrived in New York to an enormous crowd of journalists, photographers, and Polish representatives, and thousands of curious men, women, and children who wanted to catch a glimpse of the "benefactress of the human race." Marie's daughters were able to witness first-hand exactly what their quiet little mother meant to the rest of the world.

While in America, Marie, Irène, and Ève kept a very hectic schedule. There were universities and factories to visit; ceremonies,

Missy Meloney 🔊

Born in Kentucky in 1878, Marie "Missy" Mattingly Meloney was an American socialite, journalist, and magazine editor. Her mother, Sarah, was the founder and editor of *Kentucky Magazine*. Missy was educated at home and showed great promise as a concert pianist until a horseback riding accident at the age of 15 caused an injury to her back. Because this ended her musical dreams, she decided to follow in her mother's journalistic footsteps and began working at the *Washington Post*. She would later do stints with other major publications as well.

Missy married William Brown Meloney IV, the *New York Sun* editor, in 1904. In the early 1920s, she became editor of the *Delineator*, a women's magazine, and interviewed Marie Curie. When she discovered that Curie had no radium for her own work, she was determined to help raise the money to buy her some.

Meloney was known as a proponent for better housing, child health and protection, and other important social issues. She was loved and respected by all who knew her, including Eleanor Roosevelt. After Missy died, on June 23, 1943, the

Missy Meloney. Library of Congress Prints and Photographs Division Washington, DC 20540 USA—George Grantham Bain Collection

First Lady wrote about her friend in her June 29 "My Day" newspaper column: "She believed that women had an important part to play in the future. She not only helped such women as Madame Curie, who were great women, but she helped many little people like myself to feel that we had a contribution and an obligation to try to grow."

Marie and her daughters sailed to America on the SS *Olympic* in 1921. They were escorted by American journalist Missy Meloney. Left to right: Missy, Irène, Marie, and Ève .

President Warren G. Harding escorting Marie Curie down steps to the south grounds of the White House.

banquets, and receptions to attend; speeches to give; and awards to accept.

One notable speech Marie gave was at Vassar College (a women-only college at the time) on May 14, 1921. She encouraged and challenged the young women in attendance with these words:

There is always a vast field left to experimentation and I hope that we may have some beautiful progress in the following years. It is my earnest desire that some of you should carry on this scientific work and keep for your ambition the determination to make a permanent contribution to science.

Create a Travel Brochure

WHEN MARIE, IRÈNE, AND ÈVE went to the United States by ship in 1921, they landed in New York City. They kept a hectic schedule, traveling to cities all over the country. The most important stop to Marie was Washington, DC, where she received her gift of radium. One of the girls' favorite destinations was the Grand Canyon.

Pretend you are the travel director meeting the Curies as they step off the SS *Olympic* in May 1921. Design a brochure featuring New York City, the Grand Canyon, and Washington, DC, three of the major stops on their American tour.

You'll Need

* Library or Internet access
* 1–3 sheets 8½-by-11-inch (A4) paper
* Ruler
* Pencil
* Scissors
* Glue
* Markers
* Computer with word processing software
* Printer
* Travel stickers (optional)

Before starting, decide if you want to design one brochure featuring all three destinations or one brochure per destination.

Do some Internet or library research to find out what New York City, the Grand Canyon, and Washington, DC, would have been like in the early 1920s. What famous landmarks, museums, hotels, sightseeing opportunities, and the like would have been at each place? Decide what highlights you would like to include on your brochure for each of the Curies' stops.

Next, divide a piece of white paper into three equal vertical sections and fold. You can use your ruler to make small pencil marks at the

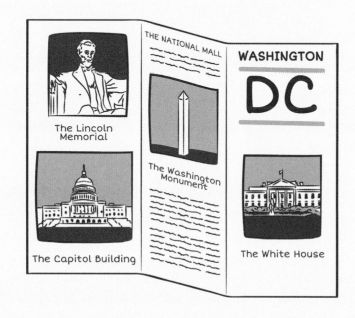

3.7-inch and 7.3-inch (10-cm and 20-cm for A4) measurements along the long side of the paper, then fold at the marks. This design will be a tri-fold arrangement, which means you will have six equal panels (three on the front and three on the back).

If you are only making one brochure, use two panels per destination. If you are making three different brochures, you will have all six panels to use for each destination.

Write or type text and print out pictures (or draw your own) to highlight special things or places in or around New York City, the Grand Canyon, and Washington, DC, that the Curies would have enjoyed seeing while they were there. Glue the content onto your brochure and label it as needed. Use markers or travel stickers to add interest.

Remember, the purpose of a travel brochure is to tell the traveler about "must see or do" places, events, or activities at each destination!

With the frantic pace she was keeping, Marie became exhausted. At one point an overeager supporter shook her hand so hard that Marie had to have her injured wrist bandaged and wore an arm sling for the remainder of the trip.

The price of fame was worth it to Marie when, on May 20, 1921, she was presented with symbols to represent the gift of radium she would take back to France. The actual radium was too precious—and much too dangerous—to bring to the White House, so it was kept at the factory until Marie's departure. Instead, President Warren G. Harding gave her a certificate of ownership to the radium and a small golden key to unlock the special lead coffer that would hold the radium on the trip home.

Marie insisted that the legal document be changed right then. She didn't want the radium to become her personal property; rather, she wanted it donated to her lab. She felt it belonged to science, not any one individual. She was also given other gifts, equipment, and cash awards that she did agree to keep though—all while wearing the same black dress she had worn when accepting both her Nobel Prizes in Stockholm years earlier.

The Curies had a few more appearances to make and events to attend at prestigious universities, including Harvard, Yale, Wellesley, Simmons, and Radcliffe. The girls took all the stops with their mother in stride, and the highlight of the trip for Irène and Ève was probably the visit to the Grand Canyon, where they rode mules down to the bottom and got a good view of the Colorado River.

Soon Marie had to finally admit she was not feeling well and could not continue with her official duties. The trip had to be cut short, and on June 28 she and her daughters boarded the SS *Olympic* to return to France. Of course, her precious radium was also on board, the tiny tubes nestled in their special lead box and locked up in the ship's safe. After her visit, Marie recognized and acknowledged that although radium may have gotten its start in France, it had its greatest development in America.

Continuing the Work

ONCE SHE was back home, Marie continued her work with radium. And with the monetary gifts she had received, she was finally able to fund her laboratory. Unfortunately, she had been plagued with cataracts on her eyes for some time, which hindered her work but never lessened her determination. She pressed on, not wanting anyone to know just how bad her vision had become. Eventually she needed several surgeries to remove the cataracts in order to continue her work. Even then, she needed very thick glasses to be able to see.

Is It Chemical or Physical?

SCIENTISTS REALIZED EARLY ON that there can be two types of changes that result when performing experiments or demonstrations—physical and chemical.

Physical change = No new substance is formed; the change is reversible

Chemical change = One or more new substances are formed; the change is irreversible

In this activity, you will test your scientific skills and decide if a change is physical or chemical.

Adult supervision required

You'll Need

※ Safety glasses
※ Ice cube
※ Small plate
※ Funnel
※ 1 tablespoon (21 g) baking soda (sodium bicarbonate, $NaHCO_3$)
※ Balloon
※ 4 tablespoons (60 ml) vinegar (acetic acid, CH_3COOH)
※ Clear plastic 16-ounce (475-ml) soda bottle

First put on your safety glasses.

Test 1

Set the ice cube on a plate at room temperature and observe what happens. Was this a physical or chemical change?

Test 2

Using a funnel, place the baking soda into the uninflated balloon; set aside.

Wipe the funnel clean. Then use it to pour the vinegar into the plastic bottle. Carefully place the mouth of the balloon onto the mouth of the bottle,

letting the balloon hang to one side so the baking soda won't spill.

Next, lift the balloon straight up so the baking soda will fall down into the bottle and mix with the vinegar. Stand back and observe what happens. Was this a physical or chemical change?

Results

Test 1: The ice cube melted from a frozen solid into a liquid.

Can the liquid be refrozen into an ice cube? Yes.
Did you create a new substance? No.

This was a physical change.

Test 2: The baking soda combined with the vinegar to create a gas called carbon dioxide. The resulting gas was trapped inside the balloon and inflated it.

Can the gas be changed back into baking soda and vinegar? No.
Did you create a new substance? Yes, a gas—carbon dioxide (CO_2)

This was a chemical change.

On May 15, 1922, Marie was named a member of the International Committee on Intellectual Cooperation by the League of Nations. Her acceptance of the position was unusual because she did not lend her name or her support to an organization lightly. In fact, the League of Nations committee would be the only one on which she would ever agree to serve. She was in good company there with other brilliant individuals, including her friend Albert Einstein.

Over the next few years, Marie's research with radium continued to result in great advances and developments in science and medicine. Irène also became a very successful researcher in her own right with the Radium Institute and was a great help to her mother as well.

Marie's health continued to worsen, yet she appeared to be unconcerned. To others, she encouraged exercise and fresh air to prevent sickness. And when several colleagues at the institute died prematurely due to mysterious causes, she tried to enforce stricter safety rules for handling radium. She simply neglected to follow them herself. She had always put her dedication to science above her health.

Presidents Harding and Hoover))

Marie's trips to America allowed her to meet with two different presidents. On May 20, 1921, newly inaugurated President Warren G. Harding welcomed the Curies to the White House. Harding was the 29th president of the United States, serving from March 4, 1921, until his death on August 2, 1923. He was well liked while in office. His popularity rating and historical standing among American presidents dropped after his death, however, when the Teapot Dome Scandal was exposed, involving alleged bribes to government officials from private oil companies.

After President Harding suffered a cerebral hemorrhage and died in San Francisco, California, while on a speaking tour, Vice President Calvin Coolidge was sworn in as president and remained in office until March 4, 1929, the end of his first full term. He chose not to seek reelection for a full second term of office. Instead, he publicly supported Herbert Hoover, his commerce secretary, as the Republican presidential nominee.

Herbert Hoover became the 31st president of the United States and had the honor of welcoming Marie Curie back to the White House in October 1929, just two days after the stock market crash of the century. Hoover's presidency will always be marked by the Great Depression and America's resulting economic turmoil. Unsurprisingly, he was defeated in the 1932 presidential election by Franklin D. Roosevelt. Hoover passed away in 1964 at the age of 90.

Back to America— to Help Poland

ANOTHER ONE of Marie's dreams was for her beloved Poland to have its own radium treatment and research center. With her sister Bronya's help, a plan was put in motion to build an institute in Warsaw. It would be named the Marie Skłodowska-Curie Institute. When construction began, Marie made the trip to Poland for the dedication ceremony.

Regrettably, there wasn't enough money left over after purchasing building materials to buy the radium (the price of which had dropped from $100,000 a gram to $50,000 per gram) that was needed for cancer treatment. However, Missy Meloney, with whom Marie had continued her close friendship, offered to help out again. She headed up a second campaign in America to raise the funds to buy another gram of radium—this time for the institute in Poland.

In October 1929, eight years after her first trip, Marie returned to America. Irène and Ève did not accompany her on this second journey, but the reception she received was just as warm and enthusiastic as before. She did agree to attend Light's Golden Jubilee, a celebration hosted by Henry Ford in honor of Thomas Edison. But this time Marie, who was almost 62 years old, was not expected to keep a grueling schedule or make many appearances or speeches. This suited her just fine!

President Herbert Hoover had the honor of presenting Marie with America's contribution to help her namesake research center in Poland. Instead of actual radium, she was given the money with which to purchase one gram. Marie was also the Hoovers' guest at the White House and stayed for several days before returning home.

On May 29, 1932, the Marie Skłodowska-Curie Institute was completed. Marie traveled

Explore Charles's Law: Make Soap Clouds

A SCIENTIFIC LAW IS a statement about something in the universe that is based on observations of repeated experiments. When something happens over and over again with the same exact results under the same exact conditions (even though it might not be explainable), it is considered to be a scientific law.

Charles's law is an example of a scientific law in physics and has to do with the effect of heat on the expansion of gases. It states: *If the pressure of a gas remains constant, the volume of the gas will increase as the temperature increases.*

Try it out for yourself!

Adult supervision required

You'll Need
* 1 bar of Ivory soap (no other brand will work)
* Microwave-safe plate
* Microwave oven

1. Unwrap the bar of Ivory soap and place it on a microwave-safe plate inside the microwave oven.

2. Turn the microwave on for about 90 seconds and watch what happens.

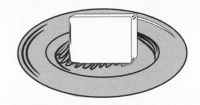

3. Allow the soap cloud and plate to cool before removing from the microwave oven.

What Happened?
Charles's law! When the soap is heated, the molecules of air inside the bar start quickly moving far away from each other. Ivory soap is made with a process that whips more air into the bar, so instead of melting like other soaps, it expands, causing the soap to puff up into a cloud.

As temperature increases, the molecules of air (gas) take up more space. As temperature decreases, the molecules of air (gas) take up less space.

Try scrubbing yourself with the soap cloud the next time you take a bath, and make new observations about what happens.

to Warsaw for the inaugural ceremony and basked in the satisfaction of what she had been able to do to help others in her beloved native land. It was her dream fulfilled at last. It was also the final visit she would ever make to Poland.

FACULTÉ DES SCIENCES DE PARIS

INSTITUT DU RADIUM

LABORATOIRE CURIE
1, Rue Pierre-Curie, Paris (5ᵉ)

TÉL. GOBELINS 14-69

Paris, le November 3, 1929
New York

My dear Mr. President,

The first letter I have the opportunity to write during my sojourn in the United States, I wish to address to you. My visit to the White House I shall always remember as a great honor and a pleasure. I feel that it was very kind of you and Mrs Hoover to give time and thought to me in those particularly worried days.

I shall keep in memory your work at the Academy of Science and I am sure your address will be a precious Document for the archives of the Radium Institute in Poland.

I beg you to believe that my good wishes shall follow you in your important work for peace and for the improvement of the world.

Sincerely and gratefully yours

Marie Curie

Marie wrote a letter to the Hoovers thanking them for her stay at the White House, especially in "those particularly worried days" at the beginning of the Great Depression.
Letter courtesy of the Herbert Hoover Presidential Library, West Branch, Iowa

Marie Curie with President Herbert Hoover, 1929. Photograph courtesy of the Herbert Hoover Presidential Library, West Branch, Iowa

Nearing the End

MARIE'S HEALTH was steadily deteriorating. She went to work when she was able, driven in a car Henry Ford had given her, but her days at the lab were getting fewer in number. When at the Radium Institute, she did what work she could and spent time in her garden there, which she had a hand in designing and caring for. When not at work, Marie found great joy in her granddaughter, Hélène, Irène's little girl with her husband, Frédéric Joliot, whom she had married in 1926.

By 1934, Marie was consistently pale and looked worn down with age and fatigue. She also suffered from gallstones, just as her father had, and her blood counts were always abnormal. She often spoke about her own death, which was an idea that upset her greatly. She did not consider all of her accomplishments, but rather she fretted about all the work she had not done.

One day in May, she told her coworkers that she had a fever and needed to go home. On her way through the garden, she pointed out a rosebush that needed attention and asked her mechanic to take care of it. Sadly, this would be Marie's final farewell to her laboratory.

Her doctors could find nothing specifically wrong with her, but they suggested a stay in a sanatorium in Savoy, France, as a rest cure. Ève planned to go with her.

The trip was agonizing for Marie, and she collapsed upon arrival, with a temperature of more than 104 degrees Fahrenheit (40 degrees Celsius). After extensive blood work, the doctor finally diagnosed her condition—aplastic pernicious anemia, a blood disease caused by her overexposure to radium through the years.

Marie Skłowdowska Curie died on July 4, 1934, at the age of 66. On July 6, her coffin was placed on top of Pierre's in the family plot at Sceaux. After 28 years of separation, they were together again at last. Bronya and Jozio each scattered a handful of Polish earth on her coffin, their final gift to the little Manya they had loved so dearly.

Marie had lived a life that included many firsts: the first woman (and Pole) to win a Nobel Prize, as well as the first person ever to win two Nobel Prizes in two different fields. She was also the first female professor with a chair position at the Sorbonne.

However, her last "first" happened over 60 years after her death. In 1995, she and Pierre were moved from their resting place in Sceaux and reinterred at the Panthéon in Paris, a burial spot for the most distinguished citizens of France. This made Marie the first woman ever to be buried at the Panthéon based on her own merit and accomplishments.

WHAT SHE LEFT BEHIND

9

Marie's work with radium and radioactivity was groundbreaking. Her discoveries actually forced others to rethink the whole foundation of physics, especially that of energy and matter. Additionally, her research paved the way for other scientists to use radioactivity in their own work, which resulted in even further scientific advances.

I was taught that the way of progress was neither swift nor easy.

—MARIE CURIE

The Good, the Bad, and the Ugly

LIKE MOST scientific advances, Marie Curie's work had mixed consequences, both positive and negative, with some far beyond her control or beyond anything she could have envisioned in her lifetime. As the Curies had witnessed almost from the beginning, radium caused tissue death. This in itself was harmful, but when used to treat certain kinds of skin cancer or tumors, it could be beneficial. The first radium treatments were known as curietherapy, and there was even a process to use radium treatments internally. A small bit of radium was sealed up in a tiny glass tube and inserted into the tumor or mass inside a cancer patient's body. Although more risks were involved, the treatment did prove to be successful in many cases.

After the medical world found success using radium in treatments, the general public hopped on the bandwagon as well. They figured if a little bit of radium was good, then a lot of it must be better. With that mindset, the radium industry took on a life of its own, and products containing radium began filling store shelves and mail-order catalogs. Advertisements boasted of magic-like powers and extraordinary health benefits for consumers,

Advertisements, like this one from 1909, tried to convince consumers that radium products were the answer for all sorts of problems. This particular Radium Spray liquid cleaner claimed to clean everything but "a guilty conscience." University of Washington Libraries, Special Collections, ADV0298

RADIUM SPRAY COMPANY, INC.

Radium Spray cleans everything but a "guilty conscience." RADIUM SPRAY is a Liquid Cleaner and Polisher, a Dust Layer, Disinfectant, Deodorizer and a Sure Death to Flies, Mosquitoes, Roaches, Bed Bugs, Fleas and Hog Lice. Will Polish and Clean Furniture, Buggies, Automobiles, Marble, Tile, Brass, Nickel, Carpets, Rugs, Matting, parts of Machinery, Typewriters, Cash Registers and many other things not mentioned.

For Sale by Druggists, Grocers, Etc.

Agents Wanted in Every Town.

114 Third Avenue South   *Seattle, Wn.*

This French advertisement featured Tho-Radia, a full line of radium-based cosmetics for women. Author's collection

and people bought the products without fear or hesitation.

There were advertisements for radium products including bread, drinks, radium emanation water filters, tablets, toothpaste, suppositories, face powder, lipstick, bath salts, and a spray that claimed to kill insects, disinfect, clean, and polish furniture without compare. The public could even buy radium pads (similar to heating pads) to be placed on any aching body part for immediate relief. Radium's seemingly miraculous benefits caused a production and consumer frenzy on an international scale.

There were entertaining radium curiosities as well. A small device called a spinthrascope, first created by William Crookes in 1903, was fashionable at parties and often given as a novelty gift. The viewer would hold the spinthrascope up to the eye, look through the lens, and see tiny flashes of light on a screen of zinc sulfide. The sparkles were caused by alpha particles that were given off from a tiny sample of radium on the tip of a pointer right above the screen.

Many of the new products were just hyped-up commercialized gimmicks. A man who called himself Dr. Rupert Wells alleged that he had developed a cancer treatment solution called Radol. Wells, whose real name was Dennis Dupuis, claimed his life-saving elixir contained radium. In reality, Radol was simply a mixture of quinine sulphate and alcohol.

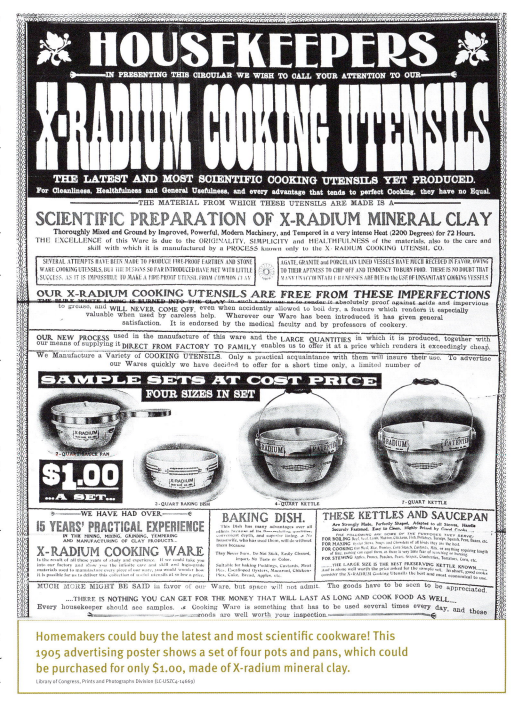

Homemakers could buy the latest and most scientific cookware! This 1905 advertising poster shows a set of four pots and pans, which could be purchased for only $1.00, made of X-radium mineral clay.

Library of Congress, Prints and Photographs Division (LC-USZC4-14669)

Before Dupuis's fraud was discovered and he was put out of business, he had sold thousands of bottles for around $10 each.

Unfortunately, other products would prove to be deadly.

First Atomic Bomb))

In 1938, it was discovered that the impossible was possible—an atom could be split! Two German physicists named Otto Hahn and Fritz Strassmann had figured out how to split uranium atoms by bombarding them with neutrons, and the result was a release of a great amount of energy. The process (further explained and coined by Austrian physicist Lise Meitner) was called **nuclear fission**. The Germans had not yet figured out how to use fission or channel the resulting energy into a nuclear weapon though.

Just months before the outbreak of World War II, Niels Bohr found out about the Germans' experiment and quickly informed his colleagues, including Albert Einstein and Leó Szilárd. Szilárd immediately recognized the danger. If the Germans (under the leadership of Hitler) had access to uranium and figured out the concept of a nuclear chain reaction, the result could be a deadly bomb. Something had to be done!

Szilárd wrote a warning letter to President Roosevelt urging him to go forward with developing an atomic bomb. Albert Einstein signed it. The result was the Manhattan Project, which was headed up by Robert Oppenheimer. Secret work began taking place in Oak Ridge, Tennessee, and Los Alamos, New Mexico, and Leó Szilárd and another physicist, Enrico Fermi, carried on their work of creating a nuclear chain reaction in Chicago, Illinois. By 1945, a bomb had been developed and tested in the desert of New Mexico. It was ready if needed.

On May 7, 1945, Germany surrendered in Europe, but Japan still refused to give up in the Pacific. On August 6, the United States dropped an atomic bomb on Hiroshima, Japan, with the new President Truman warning of more "rain of ruin from the air" if there wasn't complete surrender. There was not. On August 9, the United States dropped a second bomb on Nagasaki, finally resulting in Japan's surrender. World War II was over at last.

The Radium Girls

DURING WORLD WAR I, when radium paint was used on the faces of wristwatches and dials in tanks and airplanes, workers were needed to produce the goods. Women and girls were hired to work in factories to hand paint the radioluminescent watch faces, dials, and gauges. They were told the glowing paint was harmless. Since jobs were scarce and the money was good, many of the women felt they had no choice but to hire on.

The workers would use their lips or tongues to make a fine point on the end of their brushes before dipping it into the paint. For fun, the women and girls would sometimes paint their lips, teeth, eyebrows, or nails with the radioactive paint so they could "glow in the dark." They had no clue of danger.

One factory, the US Radium Corporation, originally called the Radium Luminous Material Corporation, was located in Orange, New Jersey. Between 1917 and 1926, it was responsible for the production of watch faces and dials, but it also became notorious for another reason: many of the workers started getting sick and dying under mysterious circumstances. Something was obviously very wrong.

Many of the women experienced tooth loss, bleeding gums, honeycombed bones, tumors, sores that would not heal, "radium jaw" (rotted

Electrolysis: Splitting H2O

YOU WILL PROBABLY NEVER split atoms, but you *can* split water! H2O (water) is simply a chemical made up of two gases: hydrogen and oxygen. A single molecule of water has two atoms of hydrogen and one atom of oxygen.

By a process called **electrolysis**, you can break apart the bonds of the water molecules.

Adult supervision required

You'll Need
❋ Safety glasses
❋ 2 no. 2 pencils, erasers and metal removed
❋ Pencil sharpener
❋ Small drinking glass
❋ Thin piece of cardboard that will fit over the mouth of the glass
❋ Warm water
❋ 1 tablespoon (20 g) table salt (NaCl—sodium chloride)
❋ 2 pieces of electrical wire, 9 inches (23 cm) long
❋ 9-volt battery

1. Put on your safety glasses.

2. Sharpen both ends of the pencils and push one end of each through the cardboard. They should be about one inch apart, and the tips should be sticking up about two inches above the cardboard.

3. Fill the glass with warm water and add one teaspoon of salt. Let the salt dissolve and set aside.

4. Twist and wrap the end of one of the pieces of electrical wire to the positive terminal of the 9-volt battery. Wrap the other end of the wire to one of the pencils, to the graphite point that's 2 inches from the cardboard.

5. Connect one end of the second piece of electrical wire to the negative terminal of the battery and the other end to the graphite point of the other pencil, using the same twisting, wrapping motion.

6. Carefully place the other ends of the pencils into the salty water, letting the cardboard rest atop the glass. Observe the results.

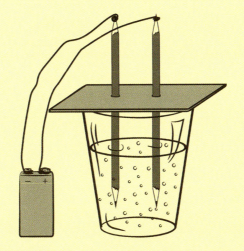

What Happened?
The salty water acts as a conductor called an electrolyte solution. Did you notice bubbles forming around the tips of the submerged pencils? This is the result of the hydrogen and oxygen atoms ionizing or breaking apart. The electricity from the battery flowed through the wires and the graphite in the pencils down into the saltwater. Hydrogen (H) atoms are positively charged (+) ions, so they will be attracted to the cathode, or positive, terminal of the battery. The oxygen (O) atoms are negatively charged (–) ions, so they will be attracted to the anode, or negative, terminal of the battery.

You just split water!

Fast Facts
Na stands for *natrium*, which is the Latin word for sodium.

While you were ionizing water molecules, you were also breaking apart sodium chloride (NaCl) molecules. The positively charged sodium (Na) ions tagged along with the hydrogen to the battery's cathode terminal, and the negatively charged chloride (Cl) ions followed the oxygen to the battery's anode terminal.

mandible or bone cancer of the jaw), and severe anemia. The bodies of the workers who died were so radioactive that a few were buried in lead coffins. Even today Geiger counters still pick up high levels of radioactivity in the cemeteries where they were laid to rest.

In 1928, the Radium Girls, as they came to be known, brought a lawsuit against the US Radium Corporation, each asking for $250,000 in damages. The five women were so sick and weak by the time their case made it to court that they could hardly raise their hands to take an oath.

The US Radium Corporation settled out of court and awarded far less money than the women had asked for, but the lawsuit did mean the public became more aware of the dangers of radium poisoning. The case also led to the establishment of the occupational disease labor law. The Radium Girls weren't the first workers to sue the company, but theirs is probably the most well-known litigation dealing with radioactive work conditions and effects from radium poisoning. Unfortunately, all the women died slow, painful deaths. The surviving watch faces and dials they painted almost a century ago are still radioactive today.

Marie's Legacy

ALTHOUGH THE discovery of radium opened up a whole field of radioactivity and scientific advances, the element is rarely used in today's medical world. Researchers have discovered many isotopes that are far more stable and effective to use in treatment. Fittingly, the radioactive dosage that cancer patients receive is still measured in **curies.**

Moreover, from the study of radioactivity, we now have radiocarbon dating techniques to help determine the age of various organic materials, and advances in other areas include industrial, food, health, and consumer products, as well as film. Radioactivity is also used by the military and nuclear power plants. Marie's work opened many doors that forever changed our world.

In addition to her groundbreaking discoveries, Marie left behind daughters who would leave their marks on the world as well. Irène, a successful scientist in her own right, and Ève, a talented writer and pianist, made their mother proud of the fine women they turned out to be.

Marie lived long enough to see Irène and her husband, Frédéric Joliot, demonstrate their process of producing **artificial radioactivity**, but she died before they received the 1935 Nobel Prize in Chemistry in recognition of creating new radioactive elements. Irène and Frédéric's children, Hélène Langevin-Joliot and Pierre Joliot, are also respected scientists, still carrying on the family's legacy.

Like her mother, Irène's exposure to radioactivity ultimately led to her early death, at age 58 from leukemia on March 17, 1956.

Ève Curie Labouisse, the only member of her immediate family not to receive a Nobel Prize, won other accolades instead. She received the National Book Award in 1943 for the biography she wrote about her mother,

Eben Byers

Eben Byers, an American socialite, industrialist, and golfer, was born in 1880 and grew up in an affluent home. He attended Yale, where he excelled in athletics. He went on to win the 1906 US Amateur Golf Championship, then eventually settled into his role as chairman of the prosperous family business.

In 1927, while returning from the Harvard-Yale football game, 47-year-old Byers fell from his train berth and injured his arm. Upon his doctor's recommendation, he began drinking Radithor to relieve the pain. Radithor had been developed by Dr. William J. A. Bailey, who was actually not a doctor at all but a Harvard dropout. His elixir was made of distilled water and a high dose of radium and was advertised as "A Cure for the Living Dead" and "Perpetual Sunshine."

Byers drank several bottles of Radithor a day, and the pain in his arm disappeared. And because Radithor made him feel so good, he continued to drink it. Over the next two years, he consumed almost 1,400 bottles of the miracle "Perpetual Sunshine" solution.

High amounts of radium built up in Byer's bones and organs, eventually causing decay and rotting. He lost teeth and most of his jawbone, holes developed in his skull, and his brain became abscessed. He died on March 31, 1932, and was buried in a lead coffin. His shriveled corpse contained the highest radium levels ever found in a human body.

Due to the high publicity surrounding his death, more people became aware of radium poisoning. It also resulted in greater product regulation by the Food and Drug Administration.

and she was also a concert pianist and a journalist during World War II. Ève died on October 22, 2007, at the age of 102.

Marie Skłowdowska Curie did not have an easy life. She encountered many heartaches and difficulties, yet she faced them all with strength, courage, generosity, and

Create a Marie Curie Vision Board

MARIE CURIE LEARNED EARLY on that the best way to succeed was to work hard, persevere, and face any challenge that came her way. Her words of wisdom are true for us all—whether scientists or not:

We cannot hope to build a better world without improving the individual. Toward this end, each of us must work for his own highest development, accepting at the same time his share of responsibility in the general life of humanity—our particular duty being to aid those to whom we think we can be most useful.

It seems that life is not easy for any of us. But what of that? We must have perseverance and above all confidence in ourselves. We must believe that we are gifted for something and that this thing must be attained.

Use Marie's words to create a collage and vision board to remind you to persevere and reach your own goals.

You'll Need

* Poster board (cut in half if you want a smaller board)
* Markers or paint
* Scissors
* Pictures cut from magazines or printed from online sources
* Glue
* Stickers

Draw, write, or print Marie's quotes at left, and any other Curie quotes that inspire you, on your poster board. Then think of your own dreams and goals. Brainstorm. Write. Get creative. Cut and glue photos to represent your goals. Add fun stickers. Hang it in a prominent place as a reminder to work hard, persevere, and face your fears!

determination. By her example, she proved that an individual could succeed and excel in life and work despite barriers and obstacles.

As her daughter Ève noted, Marie did not know how to be famous. In her very quiet and unassuming way, she was a woman who followed her dreams and never gave up. And by doing so, she made a difference. She changed the world.

Marie Curie has been memorialized on stamps, coins, bills, and even in comic books. Author's collection

ACKNOWLEDGMENTS

I WOULD like to thank my editors, Lisa Reardon and Lindsey Schauer, and all the other great people at Chicago Review Press for their help as I tried to do justice to the incomparable life of Marie Curie. Thanks to Deborah Moorman and Victoria Horst, librarians extraordinaire, and Katherine House, new friend and mentor, for all their advice and research help. To Natalie Pigeard-Micault at the Musée Curie in Paris and Michelle Cadoree Bradley at the Library of Congress, thank you for taking an interest in my work and going above and beyond simply helping me find a few images. I'd also like to give a shout out to Aaron Estes and David Dark for their willingness to review parts of the manuscript and make suggestions for improvements. In remembrance of Linda Hudson, beloved and respected English and Georgia history teacher at Irwin Academy, who demanded our very best—and got it!

To my parents, Betty and Edward McIntyre, for always encouraging and supporting me in every endeavor, and to the rest of my family and friends for your interest and support as well. And, last but not least, this book would not be possible without my husband, Chad, and our children, Erin, Elisabeth, Wesley, Ellie, John, and Alexander, who were so patient and understanding while I worked long hours to follow my dream.

RESOURCES TO EXPLORE

FIND OUT more about Marie Curie's fascinating life.

Places to Visit, in Person or Online

American Institute of Physics
www.aip.org/history/exhibits/curie
/contents.htm

This site has a wonderful, comprehensive exhibit called *Marie Curie and the Science of Radioactivity*.

American Museum of Science and Energy
www.amse.org
300 S. Tulane Avenue
Oak Ridge, Tennessee 37830
(865) 576-3200

Originally named the American Museum of Atomic Energy, the American Museum of Science and Energy is devoted to educating the public in science, technology, and the history of the Manhattan Project and the atomic bomb.

Chem4Kids
www.chem4kids.com

This is a great site with basic information and help for anyone (of any age) interested in learning more about chemistry. It is part of the Andrew Rader network of science and math sites.

The Curie Museum
www.musee.curie.fr

This is the official website for the Curie Museum (Musée Curie), which is located in one of Marie's former laboratories in the Radium Institute at 1 Rue Pierre et Marie Curie, in the 5th arrondissement of Paris, France. Visitors can view exhibits and Marie's office, and see documents and lab equipment that belonged to the Curies and Joliot-Curies. There is also a virtual tour of the museum and Marie's lab on the website. The website text is in French, so you will need to use a browser translator to read it in English.

Harding Home Presidential Site

www.hardinghome.org

380 Mt. Vernon Avenue

Marion, Ohio 43302

(740)387-9630

This is the site for the former residence of our 29th president, Warren G. Harding. The home is now a museum and houses the Harding Collections, and the website is the official site for President Harding. Learn more about the leader who presented Marie Curie with her first gram of radium, bought with money donated by American citizens.

The Herbert Hoover Presidential Library and Museum

www.hoover.archives.gov

210 Parkside Drive

West Branch, Iowa 52358

(319) 643-5301

Learn more about the 31st president of the United States and the man who had the honor of presenting Madame Curie with money to buy radium for the Marie Skłodowska-Curie Institute in Poland. He and Mrs. Hoover also hosted Marie's stay at the White House in 1929.

The Maria Skłodowska-Curie Museum and Polish Chemical Society

www.en.muzeum-msc.pl

This biographical museum, located at 16 Freta Street in Warsaw, Poland, is housed in the 18th-century apartment building in which Maria Skłodowska was born. The museum was established in 1967 on the centennial of Curie's birth by the Polish Chemical Society and is devoted to her life and work.

National World War I Museum and Memorial

www.theworldwar.org

100 W. 26th Street

Kansas City, Missouri 64108

(816) 888-8100

This museum is dedicated to remembering, interpreting, and understanding the Great War and its impact on the world through education, exhibits, and collecting and preserving important historical materials and artifacts. The website offers a great online database of World War I images.

The Nobel Prize Website

www.nobelprize.org

Learn more about the history and winners of the Nobel Prizes and Alfred Nobel, and even find Marie Curie's speech (in French) that she gave at the Nobel banquet in Stockholm on December 10, 1911.

Oak Ridge Associated Universities (ORAU)

Health Physics Historical Instrumentation Museum Collection

www.orau.org/ptp/museumdirectory.htm

Learn more about the science and history of radiation and radioactivity through articles and artifacts on this website, created and maintained by Dr. Paul Frame. Especially of interest is the "Radioactive Quack Cures" section.

Physics4Kids

www.physics4kids.com

Also part of the Rader network of science and math sites, this website has lots of great information about basic physics principles as well as quizzes and activities.

Films and Videos

Genius of Marie Curie (not rated), PBS, 2015, www.pbs.org/show/genius-marie-curie.

Madame Curie (not rated), MGM, 1943.

Marie Curie: More Than Meets the Eye (not rated), Devine Entertainment, 1999.

Marie Curie: The Radium Craze (rated G), PBS, 2015, www.pbs.org/video/2365538147.

GLOSSARY

alkali A salt or mixture of salts that neutralizes acids; a base that dissolves in water.

artificial radioactivity Radioactivity that is produced by bombarding the nucleus of an atom of one element with high-speed particles, such as protons or neutrons, in order to create new atoms of another type of element.

atom The smallest particle of an element that still has all the properties of that element and cannot be broken down further by chemical means. An atom is composed of protons, neutrons, and electrons.

atomic mass One element's total mass, which is the combined mass of its protons and neutrons.

atomic number The number of protons in the nucleus of an atom. This number also determines where an element is located on the periodic table.

atomic weight The mass of one atom of an element.

catalyst A substance that causes or speeds up a chemical reaction but is not changed itself.

chemistry The scientific study of substances, their composition, and the ways in which they react with each other.

compound A substance that is formed when two or more elements are chemically bonded together.

crystallography The branch of science that deals with the study of the structure and properties of crystals.

curie A non-SI (International System of Units) unit of radioactivity that is equal to 37 billion (3.7 × 1,010) disintegrations or decays per second; named after Pierre and Marie Curie.

curietherapy A form of radiation therapy or cancer treatment in which a sealed radiation source is placed inside or next to an area requiring treatment; named for the Curies, but the term is rarely used in modern times.

electrolysis A chemical change, or decomposition, produced by passing an electric current through a liquid or solution containing ions.

electrometer An instrument used for measuring extremely low electric charges. The Curie brothers developed the piezoelectric quartz electrometer that Marie later used in her research.

element A substance in which all the atoms have the same number of protons, or atomic number.

fluorescent Giving off a bright light by using a certain type of energy, such as ultraviolet light, electricity, or X-rays. After the energy source is removed, light is no longer produced. For example, a fluorescent light with electricity as the power source.

half-life The amount of time it takes for one-half of the atoms in an unstable element to go through a decay process to release energy (radioactivity) and transform into the atoms of a completely different element.

hydrogen A colorless gas that is lighter than air and ignites easily; the first element on the periodic table, with the atomic number 1 and the symbol H.

isotope An atom of the same element that has a different atomic mass but the same chemical structure. The mass changes because the atoms have different numbers of neutrons. The number of protons remains the same.

kulig An old Polish winter tradition; a nighttime sleigh ride party composed of a procession of horse-drawn sleighs that moved from one neighborhood manor home to another. The kulig participants danced and enjoyed big meals at each home. A kulig might last more than one night.

luminous Bright, shining, or glowing, especially in the dark.

magnetism The occurrence of objects either attracting or repelling each other, produced by the motion of electric charge.

metallic radium The name for radium in its pure metal form. In this state, the radium is a brilliant white color while it is fresh. Metallic radium was first isolated in 1910 by Marie Curie and André Debierne through the electrolysis of a solution of pure radium chloride.

nuclear fission A nuclear reaction or a radioactive decay process in which a heavy nucleus of an atom splits into smaller parts or lighter nuclei. The fission process releases a very large amount of energy.

phosphorescent Having the ability to give off light or glow in the dark without giving off heat. This is caused by exposure to light or other radiation (such as X-rays or ultraviolet light), and the glow continues even after the source of radiation is gone. For example, glow-in-the-dark stars or toys.

physics The science that deals with matter and energy. This also includes the study of heat, light, motion, sound, force, and electricity.

piezoelectricity An electric charge that is caused by squeezing or applying pressure or mechanical stress to a substance, especially to a crystal structure, such as quartz.

pitchblende A dark, heavy radioactive mineral; a major ore of uranium and radium.

polonium A rare and highly radioactive element with no stable isotope. Its symbol is Po and its atomic number is 84. Polonium was the first element discovered by Marie and Pierre Curie in 1898 as they were trying to pinpoint the radioactive source within the mineral pitchblende.

prism A clear glass or plastic object (usually with a triangular base) that refracts or bends light, breaking it up into the different colors of the spectrum.

radiation The emission or sending out of energy in the form of invisible waves, rays, or particles, including those sent out from powerful (and dangerous) radioactive substances.

radio elements Radioactive elements. This term was coined by Marie Curie to describe the elements affected by spontaneous radiation.

radioactive decay Another term for radioactivity.

radioactivity The spontaneous change of an unstable atomic nucleus as it transforms itself in order to shed energy; the breakdown or disintegration of atomic nuclei, which gives off harmful radiation.

radiograph Another term for an X-ray; a photographic image produced by the action of X-rays or nuclear radiation.

radium A rare, highly radioactive metallic element that was discovered by the Curies in 1898. Radium was used in early cancer treatment and nuclear research. Its symbol is Ra and its atomic number is 88.

radium chloride A chemical compound of radium and chlorine. It was the first radium compound isolated in a pure state, by Marie Curie.

radium salt The first form of radium that Marie Curie isolated, in 1898. She later developed a multistep process to further purify the radium salt into radium chloride, and finally into pure metallic radium.

radon An odorless, colorless, tasteless radioactive gas; a chemical element produced by the decay of radium with a half-life of less than four days.

spectroscopy The study of the absorption and emission of light and other radiation. With the help of Eugène Demarçay and his knowledge of spectroscopy, Marie was able to prove she'd discovered new elements. When an element is heated to a certain point, it glows. The light it gives off can be studied through a prism, and each element's light produces its own unique light pattern.

spontaneous radiation When an atom (in an excited condition) undergoes a transition to a state of lower energy and gives off radioactive energy during the process.

symmetry A balanced arrangement of parts on opposite sides of a plane, line, or central point.

thesis A paper written on original research and submitted as qualification for earning an advanced college degree.

tuberculosis An infectious disease of humans and animals, caused by bacteria that produces lesions of the lungs, bones, and other body tissues.

typhus An infectious disease caused by bacteria that can be transmitted to humans from bites by contaminated fleas, lice, or ticks. Typhus symptoms may include high fever, chills, rash, joint and muscle pain, sensitivity to light, delirium, or confusion.

uranium A silvery-white radioactive metal that is the main source of nuclear energy; a chemical element with the symbol U and atomic number 92.

SELECTED BIBLIOGRAPHY

A NOTE on sources: As I was doing my research and writing, the two most helpful primary sources were books written by the Curies themselves—Marie and her daughter Ève. Marie wrote *Pierre Curie* in 1923 and included a section called "Autobiographical Notes" in the back. Ève wrote her mother's story, *Madame Curie: A Biography*, in 1937. The direct quotes in this book are taken from those books, with the exception of "There is always a vast field left…" from Marie's speech ("On the Discovery of Radium") at Vassar College on May 14, 1921; "She [Missy] believed that women…" from Eleanor Roosevelt's "My Day" column, June 29, 1943; and "rain of ruin from the air…" from Harry S. Truman, Presidential Press Release, August 6, 1945. The books that follow were also helpful to my research.

TITLES MARKED with an asterisk are especially appropriate for young readers.

❋ Balchin, Jon. *Science: 100 Scientists Who Changed the World*. New York: Enchanted Lion Books, 2005.

Baughan, Edward Algernon. *Ignaz Jan Paderewski*. New York: J. Lane, 1908.

❋ Bolton, Sarah Knowles. *Lives of Girls Who Became Famous*. New York: Crowell, 1949.

Center of History of Physics. "Marie Curie and the Science of Radioactivity." American Institute of Physics, 2000–2015. www.aip.org/history/exhibits/curie/.

❋ Challoner, Jack. *The Visual Dictionary of Chemistry*. New York: DK, 1996.

Clark, Claudia. *Radium Girls: Women and the Industrial Health Reform, 1910–1935*. Chapel Hill: University of North Carolina Press, 1997.

❋ Cobb, Vicki. *Marie Curie*. New York: DK, 2008.

Curie, Ève. *Madame Curie: A Biography*. New York: Doubleday, Doran, 1937.

Curie, Marie. *Pierre Curie*. With Autobiographical Notes by Marie Curie. Mineola, NY: Dover, 2013. First published in 1923 by Macmillian.

Curie, Marie Skłodowska. *Radio-Active Substances (1904)*. A translation of Curie's thesis presented to the Faculty of Sciences in Paris. Whitefish, MT: Kessinger, 2010. (Originally published by the Chemical News Office in London in 1904). The text can also be found online at Google Books.

Curie, Marie. *The Discovery of Radium*. Address by Madame M. Curie at Vassar College, May 14, 1921, Ellen S. Richards Monographs No. 2. Poughkeepsie, NY: Vassar College, 1921.

Frame, Paul. "Radioactivity in Consumer Products." Oak Ridge Associated Universities. www.orau.org/PTP/collection/consumer%20products/consumer.htm.

Goldsmith, Barbara. *Obsessive Genius: The Inner World of Marie Curie*. New York: W.W. Norton, 2005.

✷ Krull, Kathleen. *Marie Curie*. Giants of Science. New York: Viking, 2007.

✷ Lassieur, Allison. *Marie Curie: A Scientific Pioneer*. New York: Franklin Watts, 2003.

✷ McClafferty, Carla Killough. *Something Out of Nothing: Marie Curie and Radium*. New York: Farrar, Straus & Giroux, 2006.

Pflaum, Rosalynd. *Grand Obsession: Madame Curie and Her World*. New York: Doubleday, 1989.

Quinn, Susan. *Marie Curie: A Life*. New York: Simon & Schuster, 1995.

Roosevelt, Eleanor. "My Day," June 29, 1943. Eleanor Roosevelt Papers Project. George Washington University. www.gwu.edu/~erpapers/myday/displaydoc.cfm?_y=1943&_f=md056532.

✷ Steinke, Ann E. *Marie Curie and the Discovery of Radium*. Solutions: Profiles in Science for Young Readers. Hauppauge, NY: Barron's Educational Series, 1987.

Tiner, John Hudson. *100 Scientists Who Shaped World History*. San Mateo, CA: Bluewood Books, 2000.

Truman, Harry S. Presidential Press Release, August 6, 1945. Truman Presidential Library and Museum. www.trumanlibrary.org/whistlestop/study_collections/bomb/large/documents/index.php?documentdate=1945-08-06&documentid=59&pagenumber=1.

INDEX

Page numbers in *italics* indicate photos.

Also available from Chicago Review Press

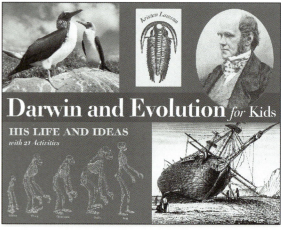

Albert Einstein and Relativity for Kids

by Jerome Pohlen

Paperback · 9781613740286

$16.95 (CAN $18.95)

"Pohlen provides clear explanations, filled with readily graspable analogies, and often walks readers, step by step, through Einstein's own thought experiments. . . . A great resource for curious kids ages 9 and up, who might not otherwise have access to this topic."

—Home Education Magazine

Darwin and Evolution for Kids

by Kristan Lawson

Paperback · 9781556525025

$16.95 (CAN $18.95)

"An excellent resource."

—Children's Literature

"Very readable and interesting biography."

—Science and Children

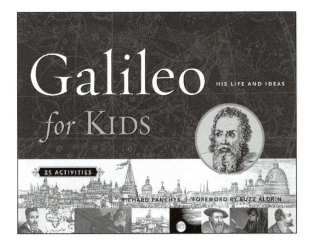

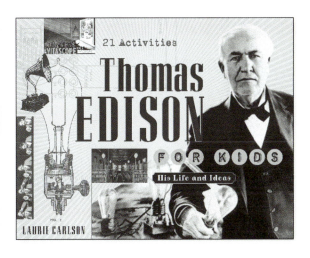

Galileo for Kids

by Richard Panchyk

Paperback · 9781556525667

$18.95 (CAN $20.95)

"Fascinating . . . full of useful and insightful information. A good read."

   —Science Books & Films

"A must-have."

   —Kliatt

"Delightful and engaging as readers learn to appreciate Galileo's genius and integrity."

   —NSTA Recommends

Isaac Newton and Physics for Kids

by Kerrie Logan Hollihan

Paperback · 9781556527784

$16.95 (CAN $18.95)

"Hollihan introduces readers to the scientific brilliance, as well as the social isolation, of this giant figure, blending a readable narrative with an attractive format that incorporates maps, diagrams, historical photographs, and physics activities."

   —Booklist

Thomas Edison for Kids

by Laurie Carlson

Paperback · 9781556525841

$16.95 (CAN $18.95)

"A solid addition to the Edison shelf."

   —Kirkus Reviews

"Approachable and educational . . . a valuable resource for units on electricity, communication, or inventors."

   —VOYA

"A wonderful addition to your homeschool library. Nothing dry and dull here."

   —Home Educator's Family Times